RELATIVE WORLD,
ULTIMATE MIND

RELATIVE WORLD, ULTIMATE MIND

BY THE TWELFTH
TAI SITUPA

Edited by Lea Terhune

SHAMBHALA
Boston & London
1992

Shambhala Publications
Horticultural Hall
300 Massachusetts Avenue
Boston, Massachusetts 02115

Shambhala Publications, Inc.
Random Century House
20 Vauxhall Bridge Road
London SW1V 2SA

9 8 7 6 5 4 3 2 1

First Edition
Printed in the United States of America on acid-free paper
Distributed in the United States by Random House, Inc.,
in Canada by Random House of Canada Ltd, and
in the United Kingdom by the Random Century Group

Library of Congress Cataloging-in-Publication Data

Pema Donyo Nyinche, Tai Situpa XII, 1954–
Relative world, ultimate mind / by the Twelfth Tai Situpa ; edited
by Lea Terhune.—1st ed.
p. cm.
ISBN 0-87773-629-4
1. Buddhism—Doctrines. 2. Knowledge, Theory of (Buddhism)
3. Religious life—Buddhism. 4. Buddhism—China—Tibet.
I. Terhune, Lea. II. Title.
BQ7640.P46 1991   90-53586
294.3'4448—dc20   CIP

CONTENTS

EDITOR'S FOREWORD

*An Overview of the Tibetan Buddhist Tradition,
Tülkus, and Biographical Notes on
the Twelfth Tai Situpa*

THIS BOOK, brief as it is, has a history behind it of thousands of years. The background of its author is the stuff that fueled speculation, fantasy, and factual adventure stories mere decades ago. Lamas and lamaism were precipitated from their remote fastnesses on the Tibetan Plateau into a modern hurly-burly world, and their coming was coincident with a steadily growing interest in Buddhism in the West. The still-fresh encounter between the lamas of Tibet and the non-Buddhist world has been and continues to be a fascinating and creative process, the full effects of which are yet to be seen. The twelfth Tai Situpa is a high incarnate lama whose life has bridged the physical transition from Tibet and whose work has been directed toward making a psychological bridge for those in the West who wish to understand and apply the teachings of Buddhism.

To succinctly explain what is meant by a "high incarnate lama," or *tülku,* is a daunting task at best, and certainly not something accomplished in twenty-five words or less. The challenge to try is particularly present today, with people becoming more aware of Tibetan Buddhism, if only tangentially from exposure to the high-profile political issues surrounding the formerly theocratic Tibet and its government-in-exile. It is difficult to grasp the phenomenon of incarnate lamas without also having some familiarity with the long-standing political, scholastic, and religious complexities that form the historical backdrop.

In a manner similar to the development of Japanese Buddhism, the Buddhist teachings in Tibet have evolved into a number of lineages which are distinctive in style while sharing the same fundamental views and practices. One of these practices, peculiar to Tibetan Buddhism, is the recognition of tülkus, or incarnate lamas. The tülku tradition can be mystifying, especially when considering that each lineage has its own way of handling this phenomenon. To clarify a little the arcane complexities, it helps to have a look at how Buddhism first developed in this sequestered land.

BACKGROUND

The principal lineages of Tibetan Buddhism are, in order of historical emergence, the Nyingmapa, Kagyüpa, Sakyapa, and Gelugpa.[1] Within these four are again numerous teaching traditions that developed in different monasteries of each particular order over the centuries. The animistic religion of Tibet, *bön*, which predated the advent of Buddhism, offered tenacious resistance to the first Indian Buddhist pandits who brought the teachings to Tibet. A celebrated abbot of Nalanda University, Shantarakshita, who was invited by the Tibetan Buddhist king Trisong Detsen, was summarily forced out by the bön priests, despite the favor he found with the king. Shantarakshita rightly observed that what was needed in Tibet was not a master logician like himself but an accomplished tantric practitioner who could meet the shamans on their own ground. It was he who suggested that the yogi and scholar Padmasambhava be invited from Nalanda, sensing he would be more suitably equipped to deal with the animistic opposition in Tibet.

It should be mentioned that in the thousand years between the time the Buddha delivered the teachings and the time they were introduced into Tibet, Buddhism, always malleable within its host culture, had undergone a considerable meta-morphosis. Within three hundred years of the Buddha's death, the strict codes of what appear to be the original teachings yielded to a more liberal approach, bringing the teachings within closer reach of the nonrenunciate lay population. This, added to the influence of Indian tantrism, gave the Buddhism of this period a richness and diversity that had appeal to a culture steeped in a magical shamanistic view. Two sorts of teachers attempted to spread Buddhism in Tibet: the scholarly pandits, who emphasized book learning and logic, and the tantric yogins, who, though perhaps having a scholarly back-ground, inclined toward mystical, even magical, practices that were by-products of the often rigorous pursuit of contempla-tion. It was the latter who gained the initial foothold.

Padmasambhava duly came to Tibet in about 747 C.E., and it is he who is credited with the initial establishment of Buddhism there. The demonic forces and bön priests who gave Shantarakshita such trouble seemed to be no match for the adept Padmasambhava. Though it is estimated that he spent no more than two years in Tibet during his two visits there, his influence was so tremendous that he is still revered as Tibet's greatest saint, and he is universally known as Guru Rinpoche, "Precious Guru." Legends sprang up about his miracles. In the practical sphere, he introduced mahayana and tantric Buddhism, rather than emphasizing the externally stricter monastic codes of the hinayana, or "small vehicle," laid down in the sutras.

Mahayana, the "greater vehicle," describes the teachings that reflect the liberalized view that developed over the few centuries after the Buddha. These teachings are traditionally ascribed to the Buddha himself, who first transmitted them on Vulture's Peak near Rajgir, in Bihar, India. The mahayana builds upon the systematic framework of the hinayana, but where hinayana focuses on individual liberation, mahayana goes beyond it. It emphasizes the experience of shunyata, or emptiness, as a means to see the illusory nature of all constructs, including philosophical systems and the personal ego itself. Through this, the enlightened nature inherent in all manifestations of reality may be realized. A component of this process is compassion, which applies to oneself and others, and its development is an important part of mahayana practice. The enlightenment achieved, in the mahayana view, is not self-centered, but it is accomplished for universal benefit. The teachings of the vajrayana, the "diamond vehicle" or "indestructible vehicle," include the body of secret tantric instructions, primarily transmitted orally. Texts that do exist usually require the explicit guidance of a teacher in order to be understood and utilized.

Mahayana and tantric traditions, while apparently more relaxed, are internally more disciplined—and risky—than the hinayana, which is rigidly structured by many external guidelines. As one lama put it, "Real tantric Buddhist practice is so demanding, it is like having to drink a lot of alcohol without getting drunk or to swim without getting wet." It requires an understanding of the nature of reality profound enough to see beyond appearances, a full awareness of cause and effect, and a total responsibility for one's own actions, without delusions. The brand of symbology used in tantric Buddhism often results in misinterpretation and can even be used as an excuse for various excesses. Pure tantrism has a razor's-edge discipline with no room for excess or sloppiness. It is seen as the quick route to enlightenment, but also the most dangerous. A learned Tibetan layman once compared these traditions this way: the hinayana is like a rickshaw, which goes slowly, but if it turns over there is not much damage done to the occupants. The mahayana is like a bus, which travels more quickly; if it falls off the road a few people might be killed, but there is still a good chance of survival. The tantric, or vajrayana, path is like a jet plane, which is incredibly fast, but when it meets with an accident in mid-air, everyone in it is finished. This home-grown, twentieth-century simile gives a fair idea of the three vehicles of ancient

Tibetan Buddhism as seen by the people who grew up with them.

Besides importing Indian Buddhist philosophy, tantric lore, and iconography, Padmasambhava apparently also inducted the pantheon of bön deities into Buddhist ritual, transforming would-be enemy demons into helpful guardians, reminiscent of what his Christian counterpart, Saint Patrick, had done in Celtic Ireland three hundred years earlier. Padmasambhava founded the first Buddhist monastery in Tibet, Samye, which was modeled on the monastic colleges in India. Shantarakshita returned to Tibet to secure the intellectual foundations of the college at Samye, and he remained after Padmasambhava left, but it is Padmasambhava who is considered the founder of the Nyingmapa, or "old order," of Tibetan Buddhism and who, to this day, is a central figure in its tradition.

The Nyingmapa lineage traces its tantric dzogchen practice directly back to Padmasambhava. The *terma,* or "hidden treasures" of knowledge, that form much of Nyingmapa literature are attributed to him as well. He is said to have hidden these teachings while in Tibet, and in such a way that they would only be discovered at the appropriate future moment. There are scholars who dispute the authenticity of accounts that attribute so much to one man's influence, and as David Snellgrove has pointed out, the bön religion of that time had many of the idiosyncrasies found later in the Nyingmapa tradition. Tibetan accounts of just about anything are inclined toward the fantastic, due to the Tibetan interest and confidence in the miraculous. Padmasambhava is thought to have died during his second return journey to India, though there are some Nyingmapa accounts that say he remained for fifty-five years and six months in Tibet. These accounts maintain that a magical emanation left Tibet while he, in fact, stayed on.

The persecution of Buddhism by an anti-Buddhist king, Langdarma, in the mid-ninth century disrupted its growth, and it was not until the early eleventh century that it made a strong comeback. Buddhism was quietly encouraged during these intervening years by wandering Indian pandits and magician-yogins, but its resurgence was not assured until the arrival of the great teacher Atisha, who was invited from India by Yeshe Ö, the first king in the four generations since Langdarma to display active interest in Buddhism. Atisha spent the final thirteen years of his life in Tibet working to bring the religion of Tibet, which was by now a distorted mixture of tantrism and bön, back to correct Buddhist lines. The Kadampa tradition was the result of his labors.

Yeshe Ö also sent and encouraged Tibetan scholars from his kingdom in Western Tibet to travel to India in order to study and bring back Buddhist texts. Rinchen Sangpo is the most famous of these scholars. Traveling to India and returning alive was no mean feat for Tibetans in those days. One of the scholars of the era who did this successfully was Marpa the Translator, the founder of the Kagyüpa lineage. Marpa's disciple Milarepa achieved great fame as a yogi and ensured the perpetuation of the lineage through his many disciples. Marpa's main teachers in India were Naropa and Maitripa, both adept tantric practitioners who are numbered among the eighty-four mahasiddhas, legendary saints who lived while Buddhism still flourished in India. The Kagyüpa lineage, then, was built more upon tantric tradition and less upon classical Buddhism, though it incorporated much of the Kadampa tradition in its teachings. It is this sort of adaptation—a joining of hinayana and mahayana elements with tantrism and indigenous animism—that characterizes all of Tibetan Buddhism and makes it unique among the variations of Buddhism throughout the world.

The Kagyüpa lineage introduced by Marpa developed into four major and eight minor branches. Many of these have not survived the transition precipitated by the Chinese occupation of Tibet. "Oral transmission" is, in fact, what *Kagyü* means, and in cases where the last holder of a tradition has died without transmitting the whole of that tradition orally to a close disciple, the lineage has come to an end. One of the major branches of the Kagyüpa is the Karma Kagyü, headed by the Karmapa. The first Karmapa was a disciple of Gampopa, one of the two main students of Milarepa. It is in this lineage that the Tai Situpa holds an important place.

In the second half of the eleventh century, at around the same time that Marpa was bringing teachings back from India to Tibet, Khön Könchok Gyalpo built a monastery near the upper Tsangpo, between Lhasa and Shigatse. Because of the distinctive color of the earth at the site, it came to be known as Sakya, or "Grey Earth," Monastery—as was the scholarly tradition that later centered around it. The core teaching of the lineage may be traced back to the Indian mahasiddha virupa, who is believed to have visited Sakya. He instructed the son of Khön Könchok Gyalpo, Sachen Künga Nyingpo, who later became a great scholar and practitioner himself. The Sakyapas were noted scholars. Sakya Pandita, who taught during the first half of the thirteenth century, is probably the most renowned of these. Phakpa, another notable Sakya and a nephew of Sakya Pandita, was present in the court of Kublai Khan about the time Marco Polo made his appearance there. Important Sakyapa monasteries were established in Eastern Tibet and Amdo as well as in Central Tibet. Only part of the original monastery at Sakya, with its famous libraries, managed to survive the depredations encouraged by the Chinese, and a great many books were destroyed or removed.

The Gelugpa lineage, founded by the scholar Tsongkhapa at the end of the thirteenth century, is seen as a reformist school because of its emphasis on strict discipline—in contrast to the seeming laxity of other lineages, which permitted or even, in some circumstances, required lamas to marry. Tsongkhapa studied with teachers from the various lineages, gathering teachings which came to form part of the Gelugpa tradition, but the accent was on Kadampa tenets. The Vinaya, or code of morality for monks, was strongly upheld, and there was a great emphasis on philosophical study. Originally only ordained monks could join the Gelugpa monasteries. Though the Gelugpas had monasteries throughout Tibet and quite a few in Mongolia, their presence was strongest in central Tibet, where they came to influence and participate in the politics centered in Lhasa. The Dalai Lamas and Panchen Lamas are traditionally of this lineage. The head of Ganden Monastery is considered the lineage head.

It is probable that the bön religion that was encountered by Shantarakshita and Padmasambhava was rather different from the bön of later years, which had assimilated the Buddhist system so thoroughly that it became doctrinally very similar. It retained the original bön mythology, deities, and demons in lieu of Buddhist ones, while it adopted a form of dzogchen, the core teaching of the Nyingmapa school. Similarities also stem from the fact that articles of bön ritual and tradition were adopted and adapted by Buddhists in order to satisfy the Tibetan people who were accustomed to ritual and magic and who refused to give these up. Apart from a few cosmetic differences, the modern bön monastery much resembles its Buddhist monastic counterpart.

Tibetans do not tend to adhere exclusively to one school or another while in the quest of knowledge. Politics are one thing, but when it comes to religious teachings, all lineages are respected. The usual approach of the serious student is to take teachings from masters in various schools, according to their expertise and the student's area of interest—much as in the West, where one might study in one, then another university, under the tutelage of select specialists, in order to gain the particular knowledge and experience desired. Different lineages are known to excel in particular lines of scholasticism, contemplative practice, or combinations of these. Brilliant teachers and saints, who appear from time to time, gather enthusiastic disciples about them. Though families may have centuries-old ties with the lama and lineage of the nearby monastery, such respect is not exclusive of other worthy lamas. The spirit is eclectic within the framework of basic

Buddhism, the fundamental support of all the various schools of thought.

INCARNATE LAMAS

Out of the acceptance of reincarnation in Tibetan Buddhism arose the practice of recognizing tülkus. This singular practice is the reason that a biography of any Tibetan lama must inevitably contain elements that are not ordinarily encountered in the standard biographical sketch. The literal meaning of *tülku* is something like "physical vehicle"—*nirmanakaya* in Sanskrit—and it refers to the coming into physical form of a spiritually advanced individual. A tülku is considered to be a functioning bodhisattva, that is, an individual who has gained sufficient understanding to be free of the encumbrances of the karmic wheel of rebirth; whose actions are so pure that they always create positive results; and who has deliberately chosen, out of compassion, to incarnate on earth in order to assist other, less realized beings to liberate themselves from the cycle of suffering. Though bodhisattvas may not yet be fully manifesting buddhas, they are certainly advanced and worth listening to. The idea of such individuals incarnating for the good of all, of deliberately choosing birth in this benighted world and sacrificing thereby their full-time enjoyment of the heavenly bliss to which they are entitled, is a mahayana notion. This "greater vehicle" stresses not only attainment of enlightenment for oneself but actively assisting others, if only by cultivating an attitude of compassion toward them. Returning to the world of suffering after one has won freedom from it is an ultimate form of generosity.

The practice of recognizing tülkus was initiated in Tibet when the first Karmapa, Dusum Khyenpa, promised to come back and continue his teaching; he then gave instructions to his disciples describing how they might find him when he did reincarnate. They found him, and the details tallied with those given by his predecessor. Since then most Karmapas have left instructions predicting the circumstances of their rebirth. These clues, though often cryptic, are found to be amazingly accurate when deciphered. Subsequently, Karmapas and certain other highly respected incarnate lamas, like the Tai Situpas, became known for their ability to locate tülkus, and to this day such lamas are consulted by monks keen to find their monastery's departed lama. After such a child is discovered, he may be tested to confirm that he is the real tülku, but often the "recognition" by a respected high lama is sufficient. Some traditions examine a number of likely candidates. To locate the most recent reincarnation of the Gelugpa Ling Rinpoche, senior tutor to the Dalai Lama, a list of several hundred likely candidates was drawn up; the list was then narrowed down to three, and these went through a more extensive examination. Other traditions rely on the predictive abilities of incarnate lamas who have a special talent for finding tülkus. The Sakyapa lineage leadership is passed down from father to son. Whatever the tradition, once the requirements are satisfied, the child is enthroned at his monastic seat and the special training for his position begins. When he has completed his studies he assumes responsibility for the monastic and lay communities that have been under his care, often for generations.

Tülku-watching is an interesting business. The ninth Khamtrül Rinpoche, who was enthroned at Tashijong Monastery in India in 1983, is a case in point. The Khamtrül is an important incarnate lama of the Drukpa Kagyü lineage. After the previous Khamtrül passed away in 1980, at the age of forty-nine, his monks approached two highly respected incarnate lamas for information about where to find the new Khamtrül. The child was found according to the information given by the two lamas—information that was identical, though given independently. At the age of two years the little Khamtrül Rinpoche sat with impressive composure and alertness for the several hours of his tedious enthronement ceremony. Once installed at Tashijong he began to amaze people not only with his ability to participate in long ceremonies but by spontaneously greeting old friends and attendants of the previous Khamtrül by name, though he had not met them before, or not, at least, this time around. He also has displayed a keen interest in the pursuits for which the Khamtrüls are famous: painting and sacred dance.

There are all sorts of tülkus. The highest lamas, in Tibetan estimation, are those who have many incarnations on record in which they performed good works. The title *lama* is used to respectfully acknowledge someone who has done quite a bit of meditation practice. This is often the customary three-year retreat, after which participants are examined as to their understanding and skill in the yogas practiced in the retreat. If they pass these tests, they earn the title of lama. There are those who continue the practice of solitary meditation retreats for the greater part of their lifetime. A lama who is not a tülku, but who is a saintly man nonetheless, may earn the title Rinpoche, meaning "Precious One," a title usually reserved for incarnate lamas. At his death his disciples will be on the lookout for his reincarnation. Sometimes a lama predicts his return, sometimes not. A child may begin to recount things he recalls from his former life in a monastery, alerting the parents that he may be a tülku. At a young age, the current Drukchen Tülku, head of the Drukpa Kagyü lineage, would play games with the neighborhood children where he enacted temple rituals of which he had no specific knowledge.

Families have mixed reactions to discovering that a tülku has been born to them. For poor families it is an unlooked-for boon, as it often brings financial security and prestige if their son becomes the head of a large monastery. Well-to-do families, however, frequently balk at the idea of giving up their eldest or only son into the hands of a monastery when a male heir is needed to carry on the family name and business. Refusals are not uncommon. The current Jamgön Kongtrül, an important Karma Kagyü tülku, is the eldest son of one of the wealthiest trading families in Tibet. When he was recognized as an infant by the sixteenth Karmapa, his grandfather refused to give him up to a religious life. The Karmapa asked the grandfather if he would let the child be raised in the monastery if another son was born to the family. He agreed. Eighteen months later, when another son was born who could take the place of the eldest in the family, the grandfather made good his promise and Jamgön Kongtrül was allowed to go to the monastery.

There are few female tülkus, though they do exist. Tibetan women perhaps had more legal rights and enjoyed greater freedom than many of their Asian sisters, but the patriarchal religious state undoubtedly placed constraints upon wholesale recognition of female tülkus. Though there were numerous nunneries, they were few by comparison to the vast number of male monastic establishments. Sincere religious practice was highly esteemed in men and women equally, but the social place of women made them less likely to pursue lives devoted to religious practice. Nevertheless, some of the most popular saints are dynamic females such as Yeshe Tsogyal, Gelongma Palmo, and Machik Labdrön. These women were famous practitioners of dharma who transmitted and founded important practice lineages that continue to be mainstays of practice hundreds of years after they lived.

Dedicated women have engaged in study and practice as fully as men, pursuing long meditation retreats in which they complete the same practices. The Drukpa Kagyü lineage is known for its elite group of yogis, the *tokden*, some of whom are still living and teaching at Tashijong Monastery in India; lesser known are their female counterparts, the *tokdenma*, whose number once equalled that of the tokden at Khampagar Monastery in Eastern Tibet. Though some lineages allowed men and women to have establishments in near proximity, in order to study under the same teachers, it was usual for monks and nuns to have completely separate establishments. Nunneries were autonomous, headed by an abbess, and administered in a similar fashion to the monasteries. The most important female tülku, Dorje Phagmo, was the abbess of Samding near Yamdrok Lake in Central Tibet.

THE TWELFTH TAI SITUPA

The Tibetan namthar, or biography of an incarnate lama, always contains the history of the subject's lineage of incarnations, because the current incarnation is seen as the same enlightened entity, though he is inhabiting a different body. There are actually hundreds of tülkus to be found in Tibetan tradition. Every monastery of any size usually has several tülkus attached to it. There are a few incarnate lamas who hold exalted positions from which, for centuries, they have exerted considerable influence in the parts of Tibet where they lived and traveled. The Tai Situpa is twelfth in a line of incarnations that spans over a thousand years and whose history is integral to the religious and scholastic development in Eastern Tibet, particularly Kham, where his large monastic seat, Palpung, is located.

The history goes back to before the title of Tai Situpa was bestowed upon this line of tülkus, to the time of the Indian *mahasiddhas*, or "great accomplishers," who gained renown for their sanctity, often accompanied by miracles. According to tradition, the Tai Situpa is an emanation of the bodhisattva Maitreya, who will become the next buddha, and who has taken form as numerous Indian and Tibetan yogins since the time of the historical Buddha. The mahasiddha mentioned in the biographies as such an emanation is Dombipa, king of Magadha, disciple of Virupa. He was a saintly man who practiced tantra secretly for twelve years before he abdicated in favor of a contemplative life in the wilderness. Another incarnation was Denma Tsemang, one of the twenty-five main disciples of Padmasambhava, who was noted for his phenomenal memory. One of the first Tibetan incarnations of significance was Marpa (1012–97) who, as previously mentioned, studied in India, returning with the lineage transmission from Naropa and others, as well as with texts for translation. He made three trips to India in all, and his biography is of great interest to modern practitioners of Buddhism. He was a family man and a farmer, cantankerous by all accounts, who experienced such vicissitudes of life as the untimely death of a beloved son, but who managed to include scholasticism and fruitful practice into his layman's routine, with the assistance of his exceptional wife, Dagmema.

The incarnation of Drogön Rechen (1148–1218) established the link between the line which became the Tai Situpas and the Karmapas, a link which exists to this day. Drogön Rechen was one of the principal students of the first Karmapa, Düsum Khyenpa, and since that time these two high incarnate lamas have maintained a continuous guru-disciple interrelationship, which has been instrumental in the continuity of teachings and practices of the Karma Kagyü. It has become a custom for the Karmapa to recognize the Tai Situpa and become his main teacher, and for the Tai Situpa to recognize the Karmapa and transmit the teachings back to him.

Two other incarnations as yogins of considerable attainment, Yeshe Nyingpo and Ringowa, followed the incarnation as Marpa. Yeshe Nyingpo was a disciple of the extraordinary second Karmapa, Karma Pakshi. Another incarnation was a Chinese emperor with unusual spiritual power whose name was Tai Tsu, who was the disciple of the fifth Karmapa, Teshin Shekpa. He was clairvoyant and was able to perceive an ornament on the head of his teacher that could not be seen with ordinary sight, so he had a crown fashioned that resembled what he perceived. He presented the crown to the Karmapa to wear so that more people could become aware of it and benefit from seeing an outer representation of the inner crown symbolizing advanced realization. This offering was the beginning of the traditional Black Crown Ceremony, which the Karmapas are noted for, and which they have performed up until present times.

Chökyi Gyaltsen (1377–1448) was the first incarnation to bear the title Tai Situ, conferred upon him in 1407 by the Chinese emperor Yung Lo of the Ming Dynasty. The complete title as it was given in Chinese is quite lengthy and is often shortened to Kuang Ting Tai Situ, which conveys the gist of it and is translated "far-reaching, unshakable, great master, holder of the command." Chökyi Gyaltsen was a close disciple of the fifth Karmapa and was appointed by him to the position of head instructor of Karma Gön, the Karmapa's chief monastery at the time, located in Eastern Tibet.

The second Tai Situpa, Tashi Namgyal (1450–97), was recognized and enthroned by the sixth Karmapa, who later gave Karma Gön Monastery to him. Karma Gön (c. 1185) was known for its library, which contained many Sanskrit texts, as well as for the exquisite art that embellished it. Until its recent destruction it provided a unique example of the best of Tibetan carving, sculpture, painting, and scholarship. It was the original seat of the Karmapas, founded by the first Karmapa, Düsum Khyenpa (1110–93).

The third Situpa, Tashi Paljor (1498–1541), and the fourth Situpa, Chökyi Gocha (1542–85), continued the beneficial work at Karma Gön and other monasteries within its sphere of influence in Eastern Tibet. Situ Tashi Paljor discovered the eighth Karmapa, Mikyö Dorje (1507–54), and was one of his principal teachers. He in turn became the teacher of the fourth Situpa. Chökyi Gyaltsen Palsang (1586–1657), the fifth Tai Situpa, was distinguished by the ninth Karmapa, Wangchuk Dorje, who bestowed upon him the Red Crown in acknowledgment of his high level of spiritual accomplishment. The fifth Situpa built the large Yermoche Monastery and added to several existing ones while the Karmapa was away in China.

Situ Mipham Chögyal Rabten (1658–82), the sixth Tai Situpa tülku, was a yogi credited in the texts with miracles that seem fanciful to the modern materialist mind, such as hanging prayer beads from a sunbeam and leaving footprints in rocks. The seventh Tai Situpa, Mawe Nyima (1683–98), was the son of the king of Ling and died at an early age.

Of all the incarnations, that of the eighth Tai Situpa, Chökyi Jungne (1700–1774), may well be the most extraordinary to date. He was a sage of great insight, a Sanskrit scholar, a doctor, and an innovative thangka painter. Even as a child he was a brilliant scholar and known for his ability to accurately predict future events. In 1727 he founded Palpung, the monastery in Dege that was subsequently the seat of the Tai Situpas. He was invited to China with the twelfth Karmapa, Changchup Dorje, but he remained behind to look after the monastery. When the Karmapa and the eighth Shamarpa died within a few days of each other in China, Situ Chökyi Jungne was left with the responsibility of the Karmapa's monasteries in addition to his own. He became the teacher of the thirteenth Karmapa, Düdül Dorje, of the ninth Shamarpa, and of Tenpa Tsering, the king of Dege. With the patronage of the Dege king, who had asked him to revise the Kangyur and the Tengyur, the eighth Tai Situpa set up the Dege Printing Press at Lhündrup Teng. Texts printed there were of such excellent quality that they have been reprinted in modern facsimile editions, with copies residing in Tibetan archives throughout the world. He was a linguist who taught in Sanskrit, Nepali, and Chinese, and his text on Tibetan grammar is still in use today. The eighth Tai Situpa traveled widely in Tibet, Nepal, and China. He composed numerous texts on astrology and medicine, and he established styles of drawing and painting that were later developed and passed on by his students. Palpung Monastery itself became one of the most important monastic centers in Tibet, and it developed a unique scholarly and artistic tradition which radiated to subsidiary monasteries in places as far-flung as Shitzang, Yunnan, Chinghai, and Szechwan. With the Dege king's sponsorship he established many monasteries besides Palpung.

Situ Chökyi Jungne was an outspoken critic of the hypocrisy and greed that was rampant in some monasteries at the time. He deplored those who violated their vows and sacrificed compassion in favor of exploiting others for gain or fame. He characterized them in one poem as "charlatan gurus" who "attain the siddhi of the fourteen root downfalls" and "sow the seeds of hell without purpose."[2] He was an inspiration to his students, a number of whom became masters in their own right. He predicted the details of his next incarnation before he passed away.

The ninth Tai Situpa, Pema Nyinje Wangpo (1774–1853), mastered scholarly disciplines at an early age, and it was under his influence in the stimulating intellectual climate of Palpung that a renaissance of Buddhist thought was precipitated. He recognized the innate greatness of the child who was to achieve renown as Jamgön Kongtrül Lodrö Thaye, the primary genius of the ninteenth-century renaissance now called the *Rime*, or "nonsectarian," movement. Jamgön Kongtrül Lodrö Thaye (1813–99) was one of the truly magnificent scholars in the history of Tibet; he called upon his profound knowledge of all traditions, from the bön family into which he was born to the other lineages he later studied. Situ Pema Nyinje had the ability to recognize genius and foster it, and he did so without making sectarian distinctions, which were all too common at the time. As a result he was surrounded by some of the finest minds of his age. He was one of the main teachers of the fourteenth Karmapa, and he was closely associated with the yogi Chog-gyur Lingpa and Jamyang Khyentse Wangpo, who became important figures in both the Nyingmapa and Kagyüpa traditions. The ninth Situpa spent the last thirty years of his long life in retreat, during which time he often amazed his monks at his seeming omniscience in managing monastery affairs from his seclusion. One story is told about how he admonished a monk to stop drinking, much to the monk's surprise. The monk naturally thought his weakness was well hidden, at least from the head lama who was holed up in strict retreat.

Situ Pema Künsang (1854–85), the tenth Tai Situpa, was recognized and enthroned by his former illustrious students, the fourteenth Karmapa and Jamgön Kongtrül Lodrö Thaye. He spent his relatively short life as a yogi who developed extraordinary powers through his meditation practices.

The eleventh and immediately previous Tai Situpa, Pema Wangchok Gyalpo (1886–1952), was another incarnation with the reputation of tremendous power and productivity. He was evidently quite a character as well. People are still around who remember him, and some recount anecdotes about his tough and relentless discipline. He expanded Palpung Monastery, which by his time was the center of administration for the spiritual and temporal needs of thirteen monastic estates in different provinces of Central and Eastern Tibet. His representatives were sent to each of these communities to handle administrative and religious affairs. He himself traveled constantly to teach and refine conduct and discipline in the 180 monasteries under his care. He was held in awe by everyone, due to his reputation as a stickler on monastic propriety who had no qualms about delivering beatings to offenders. He recognized the sixteenth Karmapa's incarnation without benefit of seeing the fifteenth Karmapa's predictive letter, which had been spirited away after the latter's death by an absconding monk who was afraid of Situ Pema Wangchok. When the letter was finally recovered, it confirmed that the tülku recognized by the Tai Situpa was correct, supporting every detail. The eleventh Situpa was the main teacher of the sixteenth Karmapa.

The current and twelfth Tai Situpa, Pema Tönyö Nyinje, was born in 1954, in the Tibetan year of the Male Wood Horse. He was born in the Palyul district of Dege, Eastern Tibet, to a farming family by the name of Liu. His birth was accompanied by the auspicious signs that are associated with the birth of a high incarnate lama, including the recognition of his birth by the sixteenth Karmapa. The Karmapa was visiting Beijing as part of a delegation with the Dalai Lama when he became aware of the imminent birth of the twelfth Tai Situpa. He composed a letter in which he gave a clear description of the identity of the parents and their place of residence, and that letter, coupled with the unmistakable signs surrounding the birth and unusual physical phenomena such as a rainbow inside the house and an earthquake, enabled accurate recognition of the current incarnation. At the age of eighteen months he was escorted to his monastic seat, Palpung Monastery, to be enthroned there by the Karmapa according to tradition. When political hostilities became acute in Eastern Tibet he was taken to the Karmapa's main monastery, Tsurphu, near Yangpachen in Central Tibet, where he performed his first Red Crown Ceremony, a practice that has become a tradition since the fifth Tai Situpa received the Red Crown from the ninth Karmapa. He stayed in Tsurphu Monastery for one year. At the age of five he left Tibet with his attendants for Bhutan, where King Jigme Dorje and the Queen Mother had been disciples of the previous Situpa, Pema Wangchok. He then went to Sikkim, where he lived in Gangktok until he fell ill with tuberculosis, at which time he moved to Darjeeling, where he could be close to medical facilities. After his recovery he returned to Sikkim, this time to Rumtek Monastery, where he remained under the care of the Karmapa and received his formal religious training under his guidance.

As a child the present Tai Situpa, formerly head of great monasteries, had to struggle to survive with his few attendants, all suddenly refugees in India. He and his three monks barely scraped by until an American relief organization provided a sponsor for the young lama. Nola McGarry, his American foster mother, contributed to his support while he grew up and also encouraged him to learn English, both in her letters and by sending him books to study. She did not meet him until 1982, during his first teaching tour in America.

At the age of twenty-two, Situ Rinpoche assumed responsibility for founding his own new monastic seat on some land that had been offered to him by disciples from Dege and Nangchen. With the blessing and encouragement of the Karmapa, he left Sikkim for Himachal Pradesh, a Himalayan state in Northern India. There he had tents set up on some forested land in the hills near Palampur, close to the Tibetan community of Bir, and began construction of Sherab Ling Monastery.

For five years the monastery grew slowly. Along with the monks came a small group of Western students, some of whom sponsored the construction of retreat houses on the land, where people could engage in serious meditation practice under the Tai Situpa's direction. He made his first visit to the West in 1981, when he taught at Samye Ling Tibetan Centre, Scotland. He made his first teaching tour of America in 1982, having been there once before, unofficially, at the time of the passing of the sixteenth Karmapa in Chicago in November of 1981. He also toured Southeast Asia. Since that time his activities have been divided between international teaching tours and his own quiet monastery in the hills of Himachal Pradesh.

Besides his role as a Buddhist monk, teacher, and abbot, Situ Rinpoche has a particular commitment to world peace, which resulted in 1989 in his Pilgrimage for Active Peace, involving religious leaders and humanitarians around the world in the effort to evolve practical means by which individuals can actively contribute to developing inner and outer peace for themselves and others. His concern to share the principles of Buddhism with others led him in 1983 to found Maitreya Institute, a forum where different approaches to spiritual development can be explored and shared through the arts as well as through philosophy, psychology, and healing, without sectarian or religious bias.

This book is a result of the Tai Situpa's desire to make accessible some of the useful, but often very technical, Buddhist ideas that apply to everyday activities, and to distill the essence of a complex subject, presenting it in a form that might be understood generally, by Buddhist and non-Buddhist alike.

I would like to take this opportunity to acknowledge, besides Tai Situ Rinpoche himself, Khenchen Thrangu Rinpoche, for generously sharing his great fund of knowledge and assisting in clarifying several points in the text. I am grateful to E. Gene Smith for kindly going over the text and for his ever-valuable comments and freely given information, of which he has an encyclopedic store. Acknowledgments, also, to David Jackson, who provided insights into the Sakyapa tradition. I would like to thank Lynn Bennett, Janet Chawla, Manju Dalmia, and Kalima Rose for their comments on early drafts. I am indebted to Shetrup Akong Rinpoche and the staff of Samye Ling Tibetan Centre in Scotland who graciously extended hospitality and assistance while I was laboring on the manuscript there. Thanks also to Peter Roberts and Ken Holmes. These acknowledgments would not be complete without thanking Emily Hilburn Sell, editor at Shambhala Publications, for her insightful expertise, and, last but not least, Sam Bercholz, publisher of Shambhala Publications, who encouraged this project in the first place.

Lea Terhune

RELATIVE WORLD,
ULTIMATE MIND

INTRODUCTION

THE SHAKYA Prince Siddhartha Gautama became buddha, an enlightened one, over twenty-five hundred years ago. He taught in India for the remaining years of his life, roaming the countryside and speaking to whoever wanted to listen to his ideas. We know something about the Buddha's chief disciples because the monks who traveled with him were often literate men who recorded details about these outstanding people. The scholars who also followed the Buddha to listen and record his ideas were interested in the activities of the chief disciples who, in one way or another, generated many of the Buddha's important teachings. The main disciples, having given up their worldly lives, seem to have been concerned primarily with the discovery of the ultimate nature of reality through the observance of a strict moral code and the full-time practice of meditation. However, many others who heard the Buddha's teachings with interest were ordinary laypeople with no intention of renouncing their worldly lives completely, and naturally the Buddha gave teachings for these people as well, on subjects that were applicable to their daily work and family situations.

The Buddha's teachings on morality and meditation are probably his best-known, but he certainly did not confine himself to these subjects. It can easily be said that over the span of his forty-five years of teaching he had something to say about everything in life. All these teachings consistently relate the ordinary to the extraordinary, and are so precise that whether considering isolated topics or complex bodies of knowledge, they are without contradiction. All of the

Buddha's teachings are impeccably interconnected in agreement.

This is easy to say, but of course it is another thing to prove it to be true. In fact, many of the core texts in Buddhism are devoted to tests and proofs of the interconnectedness and agreement of the Buddha's words. This kind of meticulous examination of every corner was recommended by the Buddha himself, and the fundamental texts—the sutras and the tantras—reflect this spirit of investigation. The Tibetan versions of these texts form a basic library of approximately three hundred volumes known as the *Kangyur* and the *Tengyur*. In addition, there are thousands of volumes of commentary that have been written by various Tibetan masters through the years, so it is a vast body of material. The formal approach is to study relentlessly for twenty years. For most people this is not feasible. Even if people are attracted to the philosophy they have not the time or even the interest for so much study.

Fortunately, the Buddha communicated so clearly and in such a variety of ways that the essential features of his teachings may be seen in even a fairly limited examination involving one or two fundamental texts. The "ten aspects of knowledge," or *rikpe ne chu* in Tibetan, is a systematized version of what the Buddha said about pursuing normal worldly activities and how these mundane activities can perfect understanding and bring realization. A study of the aspects, or branches, of knowledge can involve either a simple overview or a detailed scrutiny; like all of the Buddha's teachings, the aspects of knowledge are perfectly simple while also being extremely complex. The Buddha's enlightened method of communication allows an individual to grasp fundamental truths from many different angles. Of course, a lot depends on a person's openness and capacity to understand, because without that, even twenty years of study won't help.

The point is, the Buddha did not only teach for his monks

who renounced the world in order to study and practice; he also taught so that truth would be accessible and realization possible for people living a practical life—having careers, husbands, wives, and children. He recognized that though in such situations time for study and contemplation might be limited, there is still a great opportunity to attain realization by using even the most mundane tools. Relative reality is made up of mundane components. Whether we choose the renunciate or secular life, we all live in a relative world.

Enlightenment is not limited to any particular area of activity. It involves everything and excludes nothing. It is universal and absolute. The enlightenment of buddha is simply the realization of the essence of everything. The Buddha became this realization incarnate. When the Buddha taught he spoke in an ordinary way, but he also taught through mind transmission, which involved another dimension altogether. Through this seemingly miraculous method he taught what are known as his ultimate teachings. The extraordinary teachings have to do with the ordinary teachings because all the teachings embody the essence of everything that Buddha taught, regardless of what form, complexity or dimension he taught it in. The principles remain the same. The Buddha taught that the relative world is the means to reach the ultimate mind.

Relative truth refers to the way something appears, how it appears. Ultimate truth is what actually is. That is the most fundamental description of relative and ultimate. When we want to express it in slightly more depth and detail, we can say that relative truth is the definition of every manifestation we can name, like the beings that inhabit our world, the objects around us, and our world itself. All sentient beings, their surroundings, their relationships to each other and to these surroundings, and the particular systems or laws that govern these relationships are all part of relative truth.

Ultimate truth is the inseparability of the essence of mind and its manifestation. The term *mind* is used here to describe

3

essential nature. When mind manifests in its most superficial manner, that is the relative aspect of the ultimate mind. It is this superficial manifestation of mind that we are most aware of as we go about our daily activities. In the relative world, the essence of mind is ultimate and everything else is relative. This essential nature goes beyond duality but includes it also. The truth is that there is nothing we can say that is not a truth, because everything is what it is; everything has its own truth of existence. Things that are "wrong" sit next to things that are "right," and nothing can be what it is not. That is relative truth. Complete knowledge of the mind is not possible unless there is enlightenment, and discussion of the nature of mind can appear ridiculous, like some kind of double-talk, but contradictions and absurdities of this type can sometimes provoke a new level of understanding. One of the aspects of knowledge, inner knowledge, is devoted to discussions of this nature.

When we talk about relative truth and absolute truth, we are talking about one subject from two perspectives. Truth is actually the same, only it is viewed in two different ways, and the reason for doing this is for accuracy. Dividing truth into relative and ultimate can be very comforting in a way. We live in a relative world where pleasant things make us feel good and unpleasant things can upset us. If somebody praises us we feel very proud, and when somebody insults us we feel inferior. Some of this action and reaction is in the open, and we can see where it is coming from; but much of it goes on under the table, and we are affected by things we don't perceive directly. In this relative world things are sensitive, uncertain, and insecure, with many ups and downs. If that were all there was to truth, things would seem hopeless. Fortunately, there is an ultimate reality which gives some stability and makes some sense out of the relative world. The ultimate is nothing more or less than the other side of the relative. Just like a coin with two sides, the truth has two sides: the relative and the ultimate.

When someone compliments you on your work you feel good, but deep within you a compliment changes nothing. If someone tries to injure you it hurts, but deep inside there is something that cannot be injured, not even by the worst physical torture. There is something that lies beyond our relative character. That is ultimate mind. In thinking about ourselves, the world, and other beings, it helps to see things with the knowledge of relative and ultimate.

Relatively we are physical, emotional, and mental beings; we have desire, anger, ignorance, jealousy, and pride—states of mind around which, it seems, our entire world rotates. Sometimes one state has more power than another, and if ever we are completely overwhelmed by one we can lose our mental balance. These are true states of mind, but they are limited, changeable, and their truth is only valid in the relative sense. At the same time this truth is manifesting itself there is the other side, equally true, which is that ultimately each of us is buddha. We have the potential to express buddhahood even in our relative world. Prince Siddhartha was no more than a human being, but he managed to awaken to his inner potential as a human being, and so he could be buddha, enlightened. Our level of confusion does not change the fact that truth is truth. We can be living in a dualistic and changeable reality and be enlightened at the same time—there is relative world and there is ultimate mind.

Knowledge falls naturally into two divisions: the ordinary and the extraordinary. The five ordinary aspects of knowledge are grammar, names, poetry, performance, and astrology. The five extraordinary aspects of knowledge are creativity, healing, sound, the science of truth, and inner truth. These ordinary and extraordinary studies are interrelated, and each in its own way leads to the most extraordinary aspect, the inner truth.

It is important in the beginning to understand the reasons for investigating these disciplines. Everything has a depth which can be explored through experience. Experience develops knowledge, and knowledge gradually manifests as wisdom. The distinction between knowledge and wisdom is the difference between an intellectual or conceptual kind of understanding and the depth—the wisdom—that comes from internalizing and realizing what is known and understood. If something is understood beyond its concepts, the understanding will not be one-sided and the individual will not fall into any extremes because that understanding is founded on a balanced and realistic view.

In the course of human history, countless people have brought to light the knowledge that is available to every human being today. A careful and in-depth study of this knowledge opens up the opportunity to explore the relationships within the universe and to gain realization. The wisdom that grows out of knowledge is not something that can be forced, but it must emerge naturally, through study, application, and contemplation. Fortunately for all of us, our ancestors have contributed the knowledge that helps us today to understand and relate to reality and that eventually helps us to develop wisdom.

The principles involved in knowledge are to be found in ourselves: in our physical bodies and our minds. You may turn the pages of this book with your body, but you understand it with your mind. When the mind departs from the body at death, the body rots but the mind continues. While mind is in a body, it uses the abilities of experience and expression that are peculiar to a physical body. One of the important modes of expression is sound. Body and mind working together in human beings produce a unique means of expression, which is speech. A human being is body, speech, and mind together. These three qualities run through all of existence and might be called the three essences, or three powers, of the universe: the material power, the power of sound or expression, and the power of mind. In the human dimension, language exemplifies the type of knowledge derived from this interrelationship.

The physical body of the universe is itself very similar to our own physical bodies, and in fact, when the physical body dies it returns to the basic elements of the physical universe: as earth, water, air, and fire. It happens in all circumstances that when a body dies it goes back to its origin. The speech of the universe is derived from movement, which produces sound, as when the wind blows, the waterfall descends, and the fire burns. The mind of the universe works together with the universal body and the universal speech. We can find the mind of the universe in ourselves.

The ten aspects of knowledge deal with this body-speech-mind connection simultaneously in the smallest and in the greatest sense, and in relation to ourselves and the vast universe. This is emphasized in each of the ordinary and extraordinary aspects of knowledge because understanding body, speech, and mind individually, as well as the interconnectedness of each, constitutes the underlying principle of integrating relative world with ultimate mind. With the development of body, speech, and mind awareness the individual becomes able to experience and utilize the powers of the universe—a little at first, but eventually to the profoundest degree. That is the ultimate purpose of life.

Part One

CARING

I
CREATIVITY

*Magnificent images
will be born.*

O F THE TEN BRANCHES OF KNOWLEDGE, two—creativity and healing—are of direct benefit to others; they involve taking care of others. Creativity comes first because through it one learns the fine technical skills that will later be applied to other branches of knowledge. The art of making, or creativity, helps others because it concerns harmonious creation, which can be the art of creating a material object or the art of creative interaction involving things, ideas, or living beings. Creativity benefits others and can assist us in our own lives, whether the creation inspires, as with a painting; aids in daily routine, as in the case of a teapot; or helps us to learn more easily, as when a gifted teacher passes on knowledge.

The perfect form is a perfect creation, and perfection has degrees. The ultimate perfection is the most profound expression of the universe. The goal of studying the art of making is to learn the creativity that is the manifestation of insight and, in a small way, to imitate the larger universe by applying the same laws. Diligent study and application will enable the student to create with perfection everything that is undertaken. The basis for this creativity is a true understanding of harmony and balance, and the motivation is to make something that is needed and meaningful.

Look closely at a human body. If you observe that the person's face, form, height, and size are well balanced in appearance and that there is not too much nor too little of anything, this indicates that a well-balanced cause has manifested in the human being that you see. Causes and conditions brought about a degree of harmony and resulted in a person who is pleasant to look at. When you look at a landscape that is a vividly colored, beautiful display of nature, with a climate that is moderate and where many things flourish, that again points to a well-balanced cause. The site of Mount Kailash and Lake Manasarovar is an example of a perfectly balanced landscape. Because of the perfection of its arrangement, for thousands of years Hindus and Buddhists have considered this site to be powerful and holy.

A situation that has a natural sense of order reflects a harmonious set of conditions. This same rule applies at all levels of creativity, regardless of the type of activity. Learning about creativity—learning how to actually create something—means learning what to balance and how to balance according to the natural laws of the planet. A knowledge of these principles is essential in order to make anything.

To make a piece of pottery you need to utilize the elements: earth to build the pot, water to moisten it and give it shape, air in the form of movement, space in which to do the work, and fire to give it some permanency. You must know how to relate to all the elements and how they relate to each other; then, according to your skill and knowledge, you can create something. If your understanding is complete, what you make will be a perfect masterpiece in which everything is appropriately balanced. The function of the object being made is an important consideration in achieving the appropriate balance. You might make a perfect pot, but if you do not fire it, its use will be limited. If the pot is to be used to hold water it needs to be fired or it will fall apart. So the elements must be balanced in order to serve the intended function.

The objective and attitude of an artist organize creative activity. Consider a painter. A painter may paint in a premeditated way, with a clear idea of the particular face he wants to paint, or in a way that is not premeditated, where the intention is to be spontaneous and to see what comes out of it. The motive and attitude organize the physical place that is suitable for him to accomplish his job. The canvas or whatever material he will use, the brushes and paints, and so forth—whatever is needed—will be balanced according to the motivation behind the work. Whether the artist has a specific objective or spontaneity in mind, it is clear to him what he wants, and he does the work, balancing everything according to what is needed for accomplishing his aim. If he is successful he will likely produce a perfect masterpiece.

Creativity involves a special relationship with the materials and with the creative moment. For instance, if you are planning to create a calligraphy or a painting, after assembling all of the tools, you might meditate to make the mind calm and clear. After that, you see what you want to create, and then you create it. Sometimes it is just a stroke on the page, a simple projection onto the space the page provides. Sometimes it is more elaborate. Sometimes during the act of creation it changes. Sometimes is is exactly what you thought it would be. Sometimes you just do it and see what happens. It is the expression, signature, fingerprint, of that moment.

Creativity is a gift that comes from many past lives, from childhood, from instinct, and from study. It can be cultivated, and people who are outstanding in their fields of creativity are those who have cultivated their particular area over lifetimes. To cultivate creativity several things are necessary. First one needs interest in the subject, and then an understanding of it. Once the subject is understood, and even during the process of learning it, dedication is required. This dedication must come from the desire to do it. One enjoys the feeling that comes from the act of creation and has a desire to accomplish something meaningful. Doing it just for money is not the best motivation. It is also necessary to master the techniques involved. Some people demonstrate natural ability while others relate strictly to the method and become technically very good. Truly great artists combine technical ability with natural talent and inspiration. It is that sort of special gift that requires cultivation over lifetimes. In cultivating creativity, dedication and aspiration are the most important things. If a talented artist develops insight, clarity, and stability of mind, then the works of art produced will have great presence and will have some effect on those who see them. If the artistic skill is equal to the realization, then the creative works will be very beneficial. Such representations of perfect symmetry, which reflect in the relative world the nature of the ultimate mind, can be very inspiring and might assist receptive people towards certain kinds of realization. People who like art and go to museums may sometimes experience this effect; a particular painting or work of art will cause them to feel differently about things. They may return again and again to see the same picture, because there is a beneficial influence emanating from the work itself. That is the power of a masterpiece.

Creativity is not limited to crafts or fine arts. Inventors and researchers who have made important discoveries have also put their creative ability to work. Instead of painting, their creative abilities are focused on ways to increase efficiency, cure disease, or, as in the case of Einstein, to seek explanations for the way things are through mathematics and physics. Such creativity often results in methods of simplifying very extensive subjects into comprehensive yet simple forms. More important, such discoveries and developments can greatly improve conditions for living beings, contributing to the welfare of all. This kind of creativity can affect the most basic needs, like food and shelter, or it can produce convenient time- and labor-saving devices, as in the case of the personal computer.

There was a man with this kind of creativity who lived in Tibet about a thousand years ago. His name was Thangtong Gyalpo, and he had the idea of building bridges out of iron. Tibet is a mountainous country with a number of large rivers. People had tried different ways of making bridges, but they were dangerous to use because the materials would rot. Thangtong Gyalpo built bridges that were made out of iron chain. Some of the many bridges he built in Tibet and the surrounding kingdoms are still in use today, such as the one near Kang Ding, or Tartsedo, in Szechuan province. He was a creative innovator in his time and place.

These days we see innovations that in past times were not even imagined, except by very unusual thinkers. The television is an example of a modern, well-balanced creative result. All the available elements, tools, and techniques were combined in such a way that a visual image and sound could be transmitted and received without wires or any visible connection between the transmitter and the receiver. The television is a masterpiece in the area of technology.

Managing the environment in a responsible way involves creativity, which at the same time involves mastering the secret of the universe, because in order to preserve the perfect beauty and harmony of our world it is necessary to relate to it in a balanced way. The same methods that keep our world in good shape are used to run a factory. Mass production, where each person does a particular job in order to come up with one finished product, applies the principle of balance to technology and organization. This is true in an automobile factory, involving hundreds of people, or in a small cottage industry.

One of the most ancient forms of creativity, and one that will never be out of date, is the art of raising children. Being a good mother is not an accident; it is an art and a skill that must be developed. A mother not only gives birth to a child, but she helps that child grow into maturity in speech and mind as well as in body. In the Buddhist view it is child rearing that is creative, rather than biological procreation, which is seen as an instinctual process common to all living beings and requiring no special talent to accomplish. A skillful mother who has kindness and wisdom and who is able to maintain a balanced attitude will likely guide her child into becoming a well-adjusted human being who can also utilize his or her talents in a balanced manner. And just as a child matures with the help of the mother, the mother develops with the help of the child. Motherhood has been around for as long as there have been human beings, which is not to deny that the same principle manifests in other ways and places, but human beings are the most relevant example to us. Human history shows that when the creative capacity of the mother and the creative capacity of the child come together a well-balanced, "perfect" child will grow through their harmonious interaction. Of course, raising a child also involves the father, family, friends, teachers, and so on. All of these people have great opportunities for creativity as they influence and assist a child in becoming an adult.

When the natural laws applying to the artist's materials are followed and subjected to the purpose in the mind of the artist, anything may be expressed, whether it is the insight or mood of a painting, the clear formulation of a mathematical principle, or the shaping of an environment such as a home. Whatever form the creativity takes, it is the result of clarity of purpose projected through the well-balanced skills of the creator working with the elements at hand.

A person can master the universal principle of creation by learning how to produce a harmonious work because the same laws and procedures of creation apply in the larger sense as in our smaller endeavors. Any act of creation is in its own original way just like creating a whole universe. That means one can go on mastering one's discipline until one reaches beyond all limitation of creation and realizes truth. This is the first method of using the relative world to reach ultimate mind. In the fields of science and technology, the dream of the scientist or inventor is to discover and utilize the secret of the universe and to know why things happen the way they do. Mastering creativity leads the individual to the realization that the secret of the whole thing is in every small thing. This mastery and the truth it reveals is the ultimate destiny of creativity.

2

HEALING THE BODY

Through the balance of elements,
good health.

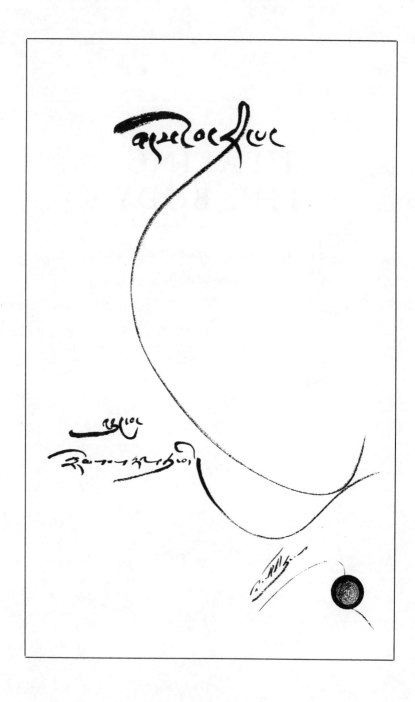

A CREATION IS PERFECT AT THE POINT OF its completion. What follows immediately after the manifestation of a perfect form is the need for continuity, because if this harmony is not maintained deterioration begins. The second type of knowledge, called healing, is concerned with harmonious balance in the form of caring for the health of others. It could also be called correction or repair, because it is an art of fine-tuning and adjustment based upon knowing how to maintain a perfect condition. The healer wants to prevent deterioration, and the principles for doing that are the basis of medical study.

It is not necessary to be a doctor to benefit from learning about Tibetan medicine. The study of medicine is a part of the curricula of Tibetan higher education, whether or not the student intends to pursue the medical profession, because it is useful knowledge that fits in with every other branch of study. An uncomplicated way of looking at Tibetan medicine is to see it as something that communicates with, rather than fights, the disease. It makes peace with the disease. The sickness is there and you respect it. You understand it. After understanding it you give the right medicine for the sickness, the medicine that puts everything in order. Our organs that are sick, and the system that is sick, are not our enemies. The body is out of harmony with itself, that is all. And that is why we experience illness. The purpose of medicine is to communicate respectfully with the body and to do the right thing to balance it.

Many people have the idea that disease is something extra: "A big poisonous spider has developed in my kidney, and I have to get rid of it, otherwise it's going to eat away and finally kill me." They do their best to tranquilize it, cheat it, mutilate it, kill it, drag it down and throw it into the garbage. That concept of illness is not correct, in the Buddhist view. It is useful to know something about Tibetan medicine, because it can give us a good understanding of what a disease is, what medicine is, and what it means to cure disease. We do not just hide a condition with medicine, by taking something out and throwing it away. That is not a cure. A disease treated like that is like a sleeping giant; it can wake up any time and cause trouble.

The perfect condition results from the constant balancing of elements. In a relative sense, everything has its own time limit after which it will not function. That limitation is irrelevant from the ultimate point of view, but from the relative point of view it is valid and to some extent "normal." The limitation arises when we are faced with a situation in which the right condition is absent and a destructive condition results; this affects the span of existence of the particular manifestation, whether it is an object or a life form. A human body can last perhaps one hundred years, but it can also be destroyed in a moment, depending upon conditions. When an imperfect condition arises in the absence of the perfect condition, deterioration takes place in the form of sickness or even death. Healing is concerned with avoiding such harmful conditions by maintaining and constantly creating the most beneficial conditions. Tibetan medicine approaches healing in this way.

In a well-integrated life, a natural process of healing goes on not only physically but also mentally. Physical disharmony is healed by creating harmony. Medicines or other kinds of physical treatments are given that relate directly to the body's elements of fire, water, air, earth, and space. According to Tibetan Buddhist medicine, everything that is in the outer physical environment can affect what is going on in the internal physical environment. Anything on our planet can affect anything in our bodies, either to promote well-being or to promote disease. It is the correspondences of our bodies to the outer world that make it possible for herbs, minerals, and other substances to be used as medicines. The Buddhist definition for medicine, or medical technique, is the replacement of what is lacking in the body with a similar substance that is available in the universe outside. By taking the needed substance into the body the imbalance is adjusted and the requirement filled. Excess also creates disease, and in order to cure, this excess must be eliminated. There are many means of doing this, but the most gentle is again to take a substance that will adjust the balance by causing the excess to be decreased.

The Tibetan medical texts are many, and the most condensed of the texts contains over 9,400 shlokas, or four-line verses, in 120 chapters describing the essentials of health and medicine. It is believed that Tibetan medicine was not invented by ordinary human beings, but by enlightened beings, and that the medical precepts were laid down by the Medicine Buddha. The legend states that the Medicine Buddha was requested by the bodhisattva Manjushri to teach about medicine, and it was then that the Medicine Sutra was given. There are several transmissions of this teaching, the first from Shantarakshita and a later one from Atisha. There is also a Medicine Buddha meditation and visualization practice, the purpose of which is to purify the causes and conditions of physical and mental sickness. Illness stems from delusions created by the defilements of desire, anger, ignorance, jealousy, and pride, which influence an individual to perform actions that result in negative causes and conditions, or karma. In esoteric teachings, the sicknesses of the body are related to the sufferings of the six realms of existence. For instance, a disease like cancer would be related to the realm of the hungry ghosts, and a disease in which memory or thinking is impaired would be associated with the animal realm.[1]

The medicine tantra consists of four main teachings: the root tantra, the explanation tantra, the profound instruction given through oral transmission, and the conclusion tantra. The root tantra discusses the sources of illness, symptoms, diagnoses, and the different methods of curing disease. It surveys the physical anatomy and includes illustrations of the skeleton, muscles, nerves, and organs. It also outlines the kinds of medicine, along with their characteristics and uses; the types of illness; and the types of cure, which involve not only medicine but also climate, daily routine, and food.

The explanation tantra goes into medical theory, discussing in depth the illnesses, their causes, cures, and how they work. It describes in detail how the body is formed and its anatomy; the causes, conditions, and characteristics of illnesses; the signs of death; and appropriate daily and seasonal routines for maintaining health. The root tantra sketches the basic knowledge that every doctor must have, but the second book fills in the gaps with important information that helps the student to develop greater understanding. When a student knows it thoroughly, the root tantra means something when it is consulted; it becomes a reminder of things studied more deeply. The third tantra concerns the eight areas of specialization: the internal organs; children's diseases; female diseases; male diseases; diseases caused by spirits, which can be physical or psychological; illnesses resulting from injuries due to accident, knives, or poisons; diseases of old age; and diseases of the nervous system.

The fourth tantra contains the highest level of medical knowledge and deals with the philosophy behind it, which goes back to emptiness. A doctor has to know the first tantra just to get by, but anyone who is serious will want the thorough knowledge given in the second tantra, specialization from the third, and—if the doctor wants to practice medicine as it should be practiced, as a way of life—the philosophy and view of the fourth. These texts are the reference books that doctors always use.

The first thing to grasp in Tibetan medicine is the division of critical influences into three categories: "air" (*lung*), "bile" (*tripa*), and "phlegm" (*peken*). Our bodies consist of these three things. Though the English words describe material substances, the meaning in Tibetan medical usage involves much more. Air, bile, and phlegm refer to more subtle principles, or humors. Air is light and always moves; it is like a messenger. The air nature of the body can take a message from the head down to the toes. It can carry and spread things. When air, or any of the three influences, is out of balance, it puts the whole system out of balance. The quality of bile is heat; it is like fire. When it is out of balance it creates diseases that have a hot nature, like fever, inflammation, or too much dryness. Water is necessary to eat, to digest, for the eyes to move, and for elimination to occur. Constipation is an example of a heat-produced ailment, where the water is dried up, impairing the body function. The nature of phlegm is coolness. It balances the heat in the body, just as a hydraulic system and fan cool an engine. Phlegm works together with the heat and air. When this is unbalanced there is too much coolness, which causes symptoms like vomiting, aches and pains in the body, or swelling. These three principles are the source of life, but they are also the source of disease if they are out of balance and combine with destructive living situations or habits.

Circumstances such as the food you eat, where you live, and what you do all affect you and can throw air, bile, and phlegm out of balance. Too much oily food develops bile. Too much food that is rich and hard to digest develops phlegm, and air is developed by alcohol, coffee, strong tea, or smoking. A very hot climate develops bile; a very cold climate develops mucus; and a place that has a noisy and stressful atmosphere with a lot of pressure develops an air imbalance.

Sickness arises when one of the three humors is in excess, when one of them is not sufficient, or when all three are mixed up and do not coordinate. Too much air can make someone physically dizzy or car sick, or can result in such symptoms as an inability to sleep; the person can become so sensitive that he can't sleep. If the imbalance worsens, hallucinations, where the person sees or hears things, can result. Objects might appear blurred; imaginary colors, images, and sounds might be perceived as real, or those that are present might be greatly intensified. The body can become very weak and feel light, as if floating. The symptoms of air imbalance are similar to experiences reported by people who take drugs. It is likely that certain drugs create an air imbalance, causing people to hallucinate. Too little air could cause one's mind to lack clarity, with an inability to think or concentrate. There may be a feeling of having to put a lot of effort into the smallest things. One might have low blood pressure. The skin can become rough; there may be hair loss or abnormal ridges on the nails and a tendency to eat and drink hot things, to drink alcohol, to smoke, to take drugs, or to drink too much coffee. Psychologically, unbalanced air can make people very rough and aggressive, causing them to shout and be short-tempered. The sharp nature of air emphasized in these ways signifies imbalance.

With extreme bile one has excessive heat, which can manifest as fever, thirst, diarrhea, vomiting bitter fluids, and so forth. Also, one's urine can become dark yellow or orange, and the eyes and even the skin and nails can turn yellow. Too little bile will decrease body heat, so that the person looks pale and lifeless. Since the quality of bile is heat and it provides the warmth inside the body, it helps digestion, and its imbalance can cause trouble there. An imbalance can cause sharp, even unbearable, pains and headaches, especially related to the eyes. An unusual odor may come from the body, mouth, or urine. Pores can become obstructed, causing boils and pimples to develop.

Extreme phlegm decreases body heat, making it difficult to digest food. One may feel heavy and unable to move easily, or become lazy and sleep too much. Lots of mucus is a common symptom, as in a bad cold. Too little phlegm causes

weight loss, no matter how much one eats. It also causes
weakness of joints and inability to move properly; or the
joints may make creaking sounds. Phlegm is actually the
opposite of bile. It is cool. It slows things down. Medicine
doesn't work as fast, for instance. Extreme problems with
phlegm are tricky because there will not be so much pain,
and the person will not get many other diseases. Phlegm
imbalance is a disease that can occupy the body, but not with
the same sorts of pain that other imbalances cause. It will
prevent other sicknesses, but it will cause disease of the
respiratory tract, among other things. Asthma and bronchitis
are two examples of chronic phlegm disease. From the three
basic malfunctions of too much, too little, or mixed-up air,
bile, and phlegm, about three hundred and sixty basic diseases are classified, and from these three hundred and sixty,
thousands of diseases can develop.

A well-known example from the treatises written as commentaries on the basic medical texts describes how a disease
arises in symbolic terms, comparing the process to an arrow
that finds its target. The disease itself has its own personality,
which comes out of emptiness. When circumstances such as
diet, climate, life-style, the previous actions of the individual
that attract illness, and the three important factors of wind,
bile, and phlegm come together in a particular way, all the
necessary causes and conditions to create illness are there.
Just as when a skilled archer shoots an arrow that is sharp
and fast, if conditions are right it goes straight to the center
of the target and sticks there. When environmental and other
life factors are in a certain relationship, the three principles
of air, bile, and phlegm become like the arrow, and the
individual is the target upon which the arrow will make a
mark. Illness results. This example is used quite often in
Tibetan medicine and it reflects the philosophy of the doctor.
Disease itself is not there, but the possibility of disease is
there. All of the same factors combined with causes and
conditions resulting from previous positive actions will result

in health, even if an epidemic is going on. When somebody you are in contact with is sick, you either catch the illness or you don't, depending upon your situation and the atmosphere in which you live. You can preserve, develop, or transform the circumstances, as your own situation and inner balance allow.

After understanding the causes and conditions for balance and imbalance, the doctor learns diagnosis. Any part of the body or product of the body may be used as an indicator. A qualified practitioner can diagnose the state of a person's health by observing the eyes, features, voice, mannerism, expression, and so forth. It is stated in the medical sutras given by the Buddha, as well as in the later tantras, that a master can diagnose the sickness of a parent from the child or the sickness of a child from the parent, even if they are thousands of miles apart. An experienced doctor can predict the future and trace the past. Usually the method used for diagnosis is examination of the pulses, by which a doctor can thoroughly check the person's health condition. There are other methods that are routinely used as well, such as examination of the waste matter of the body, particularly the urine. These are reliable methods discussed in the texts for determining the state of health, to be used by the student while becoming a master of the art of healing.

In a typical diagnostic session the doctor will make the patient comfortable and then ask questions about the patient's background, the history of the particular ailment, and the patient's opinions about it. When did this start? Do certain foods make it better or worse? How do conditions like weather or time of day affect it? Such questions will give the doctor an idea about the basis of the disease. If it is worse after eating oily things, then it could be a bile problem, and if it improves with meat, it might be an air problem. The doctor observes the face and general appearance of the patient and checks the pulses and the urine. Such an examination will tell the doctor everything necessary for diagnosis and prescription of treatment.

Checking the pulses is not just a matter of feeling the heartbeat in the wrist, though the pulses are taken in the same way as in Western medical practice—with the three middle fingers applied to the wrist. The practitioner of Tibetan medicine requires a great deal of practice and sensitivity, because a reading is taken on several different levels, with different pressures, and using all three fingers to feel the beats. There are thirty pulses that can be felt: fifteen on the right side and fifteen on the left. The pulses reflect the state of the eleven most important organs of the body, six of which are "containers" and five of which are "solid." The containers, or hollow organs, are the stomach, large intestine, gall bladder, small intestine, urinary bladder, and generative organs. The five solid organs are the heart, lungs, liver, spleen, and kidneys. The patient should prepare for the reading by avoiding extremes of heat and cold and excessive activity or stress. The doctor making a pulse diagnosis must take into consideration such factors as the season, weather, and time of day, which can all have an influence on the quality of the pulse. The body is part of the world in which it lives and reacts to its environment like everything else does.

The other main diagnostic tool is examination of the urine, because the state of the entire body is clearly shown by the urine. The smell, color, amount of steam, types of bubbles, presence of sediment, and whether it is clear or cloudy all tell a great deal to the trained practitioner. These variables exactly reflect the conditions in all parts of the body.

The main criteria for diagnosing the state of mental health are what are called the five poisons: attachment, anger, ignorance, jealousy, and pride. These are carefully observed. The major factors in mental illness are attachment and anger. The five poisons work synergistically, creating side effects like fear and violence. Often where there is a sense of inferiority there is fear, and where the ego is inflated there is violence.

The presence or absence of these factors are indications for diagnosis. The physical and mental components are inseparable, however, and imbalances of air, bile, and phlegm as well as life circumstances are as much involved in mental illness as in physical illness. A person with a heat problem will become wild and aggressive. An individual with an air problem will also be active, but in a different way—not by wanting to be aggressive, but maybe by talking a lot.

In Tibetan medicine the remedies for disease are drawn from the environment—the natural resources of plants, minerals, and water. There is a tenet in medicine that there cannot be a disease that does not have a cure because the existence of disease is proof of the existence of the cure. When a new disease appears, however, it often takes time to find the cure. The types of remedies used are many and varied, and they include measures like acupuncture, moxibustion, massage, and surgery, as well as the use of medicinal plants, minerals, and parts of animals. The properties of these materials—their tastes, qualities, effectiveness, and the ways of combining them in treatment—all depend upon the elements to which they have an affinity: air, earth, fire, water, or space. Space is often considered an element, because space provides room for things to happen.

Medicinal tastes can be sweet, sour, salty, bitter, hot, pungent, astringent, or a blend of these. Remedies also have qualities such as lightness or heaviness, coolness or heat, softness or roughness. Certain qualities always remain with the substance; others change when a substance is prepared for consumption. There are hundreds of remedies, and they are given on an individual basis, in combinations suited to the patient's needs. Some common remedies that are easy to find can give an idea of the Tibetan materia medica.

An example of a remedy in common use is camphor, the taste of which is hot and bitter, with a quality of heaviness, but with a cooling characteristic. Because it is cooling it is used to reduce heat, as in a fever, and it is good for inflammation of the lungs. The raisin is also a cooling medicine; it will help reduce coughing and mucus and will relieve chronic lung and throat ailments.

An example of a mineral remedy is quicksilver, which is cool, with a heavy taste. It is used to combat toxic states that produce pus and discharge, either internally or externally; skin and bone diseases; and rheumatism.

Sandalwood is another remedy. Its taste is astringent, its quality is cool, but its strength is heat. If you have used a sandalwood fan in the heat, you will know that the smell itself is very cooling. But the strength and benefit of sandalwood is heat, and it is used, for instance, when heat is required in the lungs, as when a person coughs and has a lot of phlegm. It can be taken internally and also inhaled. Sandalwood is good for heating the muscles and can be applied externally to relieve sore muscles. Also, it is very good for "hot" skin disease, where the skin becomes very red and itchy.

Another medicine is ginger. The taste is hot, the quality is heat, and it works as heat—it is used to develop heat where heat is lacking. Ginger is useful for poor digestion and related stomach problems resulting from insufficient heat. It relieves circulation problems, a stiff neck, or stiff hands. You can either make ginger tea and drink it or take the juice of ginger and apply it to the area.

Brown sugar, the dark and heavy product made from sugar cane, is also a remedy. It has a sweet taste, its quality is heat, and, like ginger, it also works as heat. It is very good for people who are weak and can be taken in the same way that some people in the West take chicken soup. If you have an elimination problem due to poor digestion this will help.

Garlic is another useful medicine. The taste of garlic is hot, the quality is heat, and garlic also works as heat. One thing it does effectively is get rid of worms and parasites in the intestines and stomach. It is also very good for skin disease.

Coral is another mineral remedy. The taste of red coral is pungent, and the quality is cool. It is very good for the brain.

It is powdered and put together with other medicines, depending on the condition. Coral is good for chronic heat problems caused by poisons, like food poisoning, or the condition we call "old poison," which comes from taking too much of a substance that you are not used to. The substance's heat becomes trapped in the body but does not blend with the body; it is not assimilated or eliminated, so whenever the conditions are right it can come up again—just as when you eat too much of something once and get sick, and then it makes you sick every time you eat it after that.

The taste of coal is hot and pungent together. The quality is heat. It is very good for some kinds of nervous problems, such as when one's nerves are overworked or what we call too open. Medicine made with coal helps treat stony accumulations, like gall stones or kidney stones, by breaking them up.

One very pleasant medicine is honey. The taste is sweet and the quality is heat. Honey is very good for the skin and the eyes, and for health generally, so it is good to have honey from time to time.

Those are just a few of the vast number of medicines that are made by preparing and combining natural things in different ways. There are other unusual and exotic remedies—rare plants and parts of animals—but medicine often consists of very ordinary things, like those mentioned. Of course, most of these medicines require special preparation. They cannot all be taken in their natural form because some are poisonous and the poison must be neutralized in a way that preserves the strength of the remedy. Raw materials from animal, vegetable, or mineral sources are treated in various ways to purify them, even if they are perfectly safe, in order to make them suitable for medical use. After being refined in the appropriate way, the substances are often combined to make different medicines, some of which are standard preparations. The most important factor in making up a medicine, however, is the individual's need. Careful preparation of medicine according to the pharmacological texts, which every healer must learn, is time-consuming, and each patient must be treated with individual attention, because even though there might be a hundred people with the same disease, the manifestation of the disease and therefore the remedy may be slightly different in each case.

In addition to prescribing medicines, the doctor may prescribe physical treatments like massage, moxibustion, or hot water baths. Hot water therapy has a special place in Tibetan medicine. It is usually used for deep-seated diseases like bone disease, as well as for muscle, blood, and skin diseases, but not so much for diseases of the organs. The best source of water for this therapy is natural hot springs. In Tibet there are many hot springs; in one famous place there are over one hundred. Many of the springs have a distinctive taste and smell, due to their mineral content, and on each there is a marker telling what ailment it is good for. Hot springs water containing sulphur can be identified by its yellowish color, bitter taste, and characteristic smell. Sulphur is very good for leprosy, which is one of the most difficult diseases to cure in Tibetan medicine. Calcite springs are good for cold diseases, like rheumatism, and also skin disease. Limestone springs have yet other benefits. Combinations of these minerals also can be used.

When hot tub treatment is given, strict guidelines are followed. A solution like barley wine, which is 40 percent medicine and 60 percent barley, is used in the bath. The bath may be applied to isolated parts of the body or the whole body. Maximum treatment is three weeks, no more than one hour at a time, and the number of baths a day varies according to the condition of the patient. The important thing to consider is the state of the heart. At first the person does not spend much time in the bath, and the water is not hotter than the person is comfortable in. The amount of medicine and heat are increased gradually, and then decreased just as gradually. A course of therapy might consist of ten days of increasing, one day at the peak, and ten days of decreasing. For such ailments as skin, bone, and muscle diseases, the bath is much better than taking medicine orally because it penetrates the body from the outside in, so the surface of the body becomes like the walls of the intestines, assimilating the medicine very effectively.

This brief outline of some of the major points of Tibetan medical theory and the treatment of physical disorders is meant to convey some of the fundamental principles of healing. When the knowledge of healing is applied, the process of maintaining a perfect balance can continue to be refined until there is a spontaneous harmony taking place ceaselessly. This perfection of conditions can be called immortality. It is an advanced state in which every part of the physical system operates in automatic, continuous harmony and balance. Having our physical bodies in harmony is an important step toward balance in our relative world; it is a state that will enable us more easily to approach the realization of ultimate mind.

3
HEALING
THE MIND

Mind is the essence of everything.
Due to mind's purity, all becomes pure.
Due to mind's clarity, all becomes clear.
Due to mind's well-being, all becomes well.
The essence of everything is one's own mind.

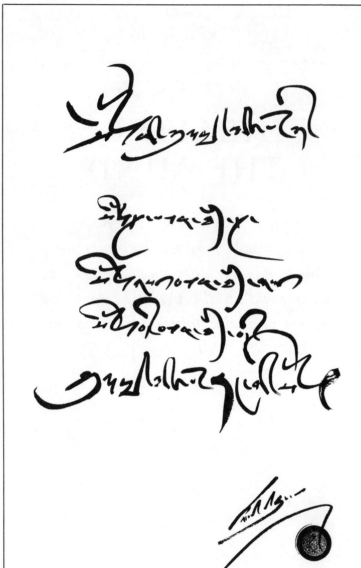

ALTHOUGH PHYSICAL IMBALANCE IS A serious condition, mental disharmony is the more serious affliction. The same principles of diagnosis and treatment apply in mental illness as in physical illness because the health of the mind in the ordinary sense is just like the health of the body, and that which is out of balance needs to be balanced. Perfect mental balance on the relative level involves equalizing desire, anger, ignorance, jealousy, and pride. These factors will always be there in the relative world, so finding and maintaining their perfect balance is the essential thing. Mental health can be maintained by keeping these mental poisons in line, without letting any of them get out of control. If there is a major imbalance of these factors, illness results, and a person is overwhelmed with confusion about what he or she perceives as reality. Balance rests upon maintaining clarity amid the confusion pervading human life.

The art of healing body and the art of healing mind go together. Mental illness is treated, in the Tibetan medical tradition, with medicines, physical therapy, and recommendations for diet and daily activities, just as physical illness is. Treatment may also include special techniques for the mind itself, which today might be termed psychotherapy. Before beginning to discuss therapy and therapeutic techniques it must be made clear that the perspective of a Tibetan on the subject will be somewhat different from that of a Westerner. It is important to understand this difference before proceeding into any discussion of therapy.

Therapy is a concept and practice that has developed as a result of the kinds of lives that many people lead in the fast-moving, high-tech societies of today. In Tibet there were no therapists such as there are in the West. There is, though, a kind of therapy in Buddhist religion, education, and family life. Just by living in a completely natural setting a person goes through a gentle therapeutic process. Nowadays, in many countries of the world, the practice of psychotherapy has arisen in response to a need created by life-styles and social roles that are different from the old, traditional ones. When people are not exposed to the natural process of life and are isolated from a natural reality, therapy becomes more necessary as a means to handle stress in the new situation.

The early part of life is the most important for forming attitudes and responses. This process begins with conception and continues while a person is growing from a helpless newborn baby into an independent, adult human being. During this period, which is roughly twenty years, a person's outlook is not only formed but deeply rooted by experiences. Those experiences come out of the environment.

Confusion and emotional or physical difficulties in the life of a pregnant woman will have an effect on the child she is carrying. Where people live close to nature they become aware of such factors without really trying. It is not necessary to make a special study of it in an environment where all natural phenomena are experienced and accepted. In developed societies in which people grow up in cities, they are apt to stop listening to natural rhythms, and such simple facts of life often must be rediscovered. In Tibetan custom, when the mother is carrying the child in her body, her condition is respected and people make efforts to minimize her physical and mental stress. After birth, the family structure and way of life support the child physically, emotionally, and mentally. The natural pattern, where grandparents, uncles, aunts, and cousins, in addition to the father and mother, take care of the child's needs, provides stability within the natural environment. These people don't have shopping centers, big highways, and so on. They live with nature, and they know the trees, flowers, and animals. The child sees his mother milking the cow to get the milk that he is going to drink for breakfast.

From the beginning he learns about the natural order of things from nature itself. A typical middle-class Tibetan family has two places to live: a highland estate for the summers and a lowland estate for the winters. The family has seasonal separations and reunions, since some family members stay mostly in one place, but most of the younger adults move back and forth. They experience sadness at parting and happiness at the real communication that takes place at meeting their friends and relatives once again.

Tibetan children get plenty of care from all their relatives, who create a loving circle of attention as well as a circle of discipline. They are exposed to natural reality all of the time. If they see a death, it is real death. When an animal dies, or one of their relatives dies, or they see somebody sick, they experience the real thing, firsthand. Death is not something that appears on a square screen, acted out by people who then get up and star in another movie. That is not the kind of illusion they grow up in. A common practice is for a parent to tell a child who does not want to eat her yogurt to please take three more spoonfuls for the sake of such-and-such cow who gives the milk, and that way the child learns where yogurt comes from. A child knows whether her jacket is made out of wool from the sheep, the very fine hair of the goat, or the skin or fur of some other animal. She saw how it was made by her mother or uncle, and maybe she helped clean, separate, or spin the wool.

This kind of natural information has a deeper value that relates to a person's inner development. When someone learns that it is necessary to wait half a year for certain flowers to grow, having watched them grow from seeds into plants, and having watched the leaves come out and buds open up—all in a certain, reliable period of time—an appreciation of the natural rhythm of things develops. One becomes aware at a deep level that things happen in a particular way and at the right time. This sort of appreciation builds the ability to accept other kinds of circumstances as they occur throughout life. It helps a person understand the temporary nature of life and its phases.

It takes time to grow into an adult; it takes time to discover how things function. Through the process of growing up surrounded by nature, these relative laws become clearer. One understands the fundamentals, so there isn't a need for a therapist to explain things. When truthful, accurate, and clear information is given kindly in a peaceful environment, then one is likely to become a kind, patient person with some understanding of the natural way things work. This is not to say nobody will be confused, or that there will be no crazy people, but there will be much, much less of the sorts of emotional upheavals that people are now experiencing in developed countries.

Development is not a bad thing, but the problem is that the development we see around us has happened so fast. Even in the most thoroughly modern countries, things have not been advanced for very long. It is a recent phenomenon, which took place in the last hundred years or less. If you compare how much change has occurred in the last hundred years with how much occurred before that, it seems incredible; the recent period of change is equivalent to maybe several thousand years of previous change. The natural way of life went on with slow developments over millions of years, until it suddenly speeded up.

If we are honest with ourselves, we should be happy that we are not all in a state of total nervous breakdown or insanity. We should be happy that we are okay. We are going fast, but we have somehow been able to catch up. It is this situation, though, that has brought the development of psychology and psychotherapy. People who grow up in a changed, more artificial environment have difficulty understanding that life is simple. Everything becomes very complicated for them, especially such things as love, caring for themselves and other people, having balanced relationships, discipline, and so forth. Such basic states as happiness, sadness, death, and birth all become very complicated. Even though they might have a lot of materials to learn from, like books and video cassettes that discuss every critical aspect of life, it is indirect learning. They may read a hundred books and still be confused. People who have grown up with nature might not have seen any books, and they might not have the ability to explain what love, respect, or kindness is, but they know and feel these principles in a way that gives them stability. The professional therapist has originated from the need of modern people to find answers for all those major questions that didn't need to be asked in the past. Nowadays the simple things that people once knew naturally have become areas of uncertainty.

Cultural influences create noticeable differences in the way people behave. Polish, Spanish, Greek, English, American, Chinese, Indian, and French people all have their own ways of looking at things because of their cultural backgrounds. Easterners and Occidentals have perspectives that are so different that it is sometimes difficult for them to understand each other. This is not a negative or positive thing; it is just a fact. Tibetans rarely show emotion, for instance, but in many Western cultures it is considered appropriate to be emotionally demonstrative. An Indian might ask a total stranger a lot of personal questions, which in India is a usual way to behave but to a Westerner might seem very rude. A Westerner's directness, however, could offend an Indian just as much. In the '60s and '70s, when so many young Westerners came to India to learn Eastern philosophy, it was interesting that though they may have come from well-off families, they went around in old clothes, without cameras, even without shoes. To people in a country where so many have to go around like that, and have no choice, it seemed strange; it was hard to understand. Of course, these Westerners had come from technologically advanced countries where there was material prosperity, but in which they felt a lack of spiritual values.

41

They had been cut off from certain experiences of reality which they tried to find in India.

Regardless of culture, however, the essential nature of the mind is the same for everybody. The elements of people's relative reality are the same and so are the principles that govern it. Cultural differences, as well as individual differences, are part of the infinitely variable cycle of change and manifestation of phenomena, in Buddhism called samsara.[1] All situations, events, personality types, motivations, attitudes, balances, and imbalances are part of this, whatever society a person may have grown up in. These patterns change constantly, though they are based on the five main themes of desire, anger, ignorance, jealousy, and pride.

Out of all the negative attitudes that are common today, one of the most destructive is self-hate. There seem to be many people who hate themselves. This is hard for someone coming from the Tibetan Buddhist culture to understand, where it is an accepted fact that everyone likes themselves too much, certainly more than anything else. The generally held view is that all problems come from being too attached to oneself, so that practices have evolved that develop more concern for the well-being of others as well as oneself. Buddhist teachings emphasize the suffering of life and how suffering is created, in order to modify the focus on "I," "myself," which perpetuates a lack of awareness or concern for anything beyond the likes and dislikes of the self. The emphasis on suffering is not to make people feel bad about themselves, but to help them feel better about their situation by being realistic about it. Being realistic helps people to accept themselves and their situation honestly so they can then work to improve it. They can feel better about what they are rather than letting suffering become a cause for more negativity in their lives. By facing up to their defects of anger, ignorance, jealousy, desire, and pride, and by acknowledging that suffering comes from those states, they can become more objective about their relative world.

These observations regarding modern psychology, it should be clear, come from growing up as Tibetan in India, particularly in the Himalayan regions of Sikkim and Darjeeling, and from having exposure to many people from different backgrounds, both Asian and Western. These opinions are not based on any training in modern Western psychology, but on some training in what a Westerner might call Buddhist psychology.

There is an important tenet of Buddhism that can act therapeutically for people who have a problem accepting themselves as they are. People usually get upset with themselves because they cannot live up to their idea of what they want to be. They see their weaknesses and problems, and this depresses them. Actually, to see your faults is beneficial. It is better than not seeing them. However, when you see your limitations, your problems, and your weaknesses as the ultimate aspect of yourself, you can become extremely negative about yourself and everything around you. In the teaching of the Buddha there is no negativity that is ultimate; there is no weakness that is ultimate. All negativity, shortcomings, and problems are relative and temporary. Ultimately everything is perfect. There is no imperfection in the ultimate sense. To know and understand that can help people to stop saying they hate themselves. No matter how many mistakes human beings might make, the ultimate nature of every human being is perfect and positive. It is beyond the body, personality, and changing circumstances of any particular life.

If you don't know that your ultimate potential is perfect, you will want to hide your weakness, not only from others but from yourself. Some people do this with psychological games, and others with self-destructive habits. People who believe that their own negativity is the whole story are susceptible to becoming even worse—to becoming alcoholics or drug addicts, or to developing forms of insanity—in their attempts to ignore their imperfect relative reality. Who wants to admit that they are ultimately bad? If you see your weakness as your ultimate potential, you are finished; there is no hope, no possibility to improve anything. When you understand that your shortcomings are relative and changeable, and that it is possible to manifest your ultimate potential, there comes a realistic confidence in who you are. That is how you can become a person who is open while at the same time practical, motivated, and effective. There will be real, tangible benefit because you will be involved in your life while having a total trust in, and understanding of, your ultimate enlightened nature. Relatively, of course, you are not perfect, so you always have to watch out, be mindful, and learn more so you can bring out more of your beneficial ultimate nature, even though ultimately you are perfect. It is a paradox, but it is a paradox that is helpful to contemplate and understand.

There is a Buddhist practice that does some of the same things that therapy is designed to do. That practice is meditation. Buddhist prayer might also be seen as therapy. Even living life according to certain guidelines is therapeutic. Meditation is a deep and powerful thing. It is not superficial and does not necessarily answer all one's questions, just like that. It is subtler than that. Meditation is a method of helping a person to simply dissolve the questions. The answers that are important to know are understood, felt, or realized.

Since it is not practical to think that the world will go back to a state where everyone lives close to nature, in countries where it is no longer possible to grow up in a healthy, peaceful, and natural way, people need methods that will help them find a true and natural understanding of reality. For many people this may involve therapy, and for others, meditation. The methods in Tibetan Buddhism that are used for healing the mind might be used as a kind of therapy, though they have not been traditionally considered therapy, as that term is used today.

From a Buddhist perspective, there seem to be two extreme approaches to life. Of course, many people fall somewhere between these two extremes, having characteristics of one or the other and sometimes both extremes. At one end are the people who are big on the past and future life, but who have almost no focus on the present. Such a person's time is consumed by considering why things happened the way they did or by making plans for the future. At the other end of the extreme are those who are absolutely closed to the possibility of a future or a past beyond this life; life is like a piece of solid wood cut at both ends. The person in this category can be sane, insane, happy, depressed, whatever, but feels that life begins with birth, ends with death, and that's it. Both of these extreme types have a great deal of resentment and insecurity.

There is a positive side to such orientations. The people who question the past and look ahead to the future are very open. They are ready to understand many things in some depth. They are something like magnets. Things that can otherwise be difficult to understand and accept can be assimilated by these people easily. When they accomplish something good, they don't make too big a deal about it because they are always looking ahead for something better; in this way they do not cling so much to what they have now. That allows them to move ahead, which is very good. They do not get stuck by being content with what they have in the present, but always see what they don't have.

The solid type of people tend to be extremely efficient, and when they do something they finish it. Their way of accomplishing a task is to act with a lot of power, almost as if they were smashing something. They can really get things done. They are very sure of themselves and have no hesitation once they are involved. When they do something they sit on top of it until it is finished, quite confident of their right to take control. They often do not show emotions that much, even though they feel them.

As is true in any society, certain things are expected from a Tibetan Buddhist in order for that person to earn respect. There are ideals people try to live up to, such as being of benefit not only to themselves but to others. They develop their capacity to benefit others and try to put themselves in another's place to increase their understanding. When people are religious or inclined toward deeper things, they aim for enlightenment, not just limiting themselves to perfecting their conduct as human beings, which is only a step on the path to complete enlightenment. Buddhism explains the possibility of enlightenment and also how to reach it. Enlightenment is total realization, beyond any limitation. Physical perfection is not so important. The most important thing is perfect mind and mental capability. Mr. and Miss Universe don't have a place in the Tibetan worldview.

Human beings fall into three categories. In the first category are "perfect" human beings who are good for themselves and for those they associate with, and whose actions are constructive. The second category comprises people who are good for themselves but not so beneficial for others, though they are not harmful to others. The third category comprises those who are bad for themselves and bad for everyone. The perfect type of human being can change and grow worse, and the weak, imperfect human being can improve. These classifications are not permanent, but relative and temporary.

Clarity of the mind provides the cause. If your mind is clear then you can be a perfect human being. If your mind is confused, you might be in the second or maybe even in the third category. There are many methods to clarify the mind that can be applied from the time of birth until a person breathes his last breath. They do not work in the same way for everyone. If someone has an established habit of negative behavior, then moving up to being a good or even a harmless person will be difficult and will take a lot of effort. A negative condition may be caused by temporary circumstances, such as when a wonderful person has many difficulties and problems. If the person does not have a deep habit of negativity, then the negative states of mind brought up by life's problems may be overcome much more easily. If a person becomes beneficial for himself and everyone else by putting genuine effort into developing that positive habit, then it will remain firmly and will be very difficult to change for the worse. However, if a person falls into the first category because of lucky circumstances, delusions can arise and the situation can change very easily.

These characteristic types have distinctive qualities. The best person's heart is said to be like space, very big. Space can accommodate everything; the whole universe can exist in space. The truly good person's heart is so open and vast that he or she can stand any kind of situation and condition. The second type of person is like a country. There is space for certain things, but there are borders, so there is a kind of limitation. The person in the third category is said to have a mind like a small, well-decorated room, full of bric-a-brac. There isn't much room for anything except clutter. These states of mind can be altered, however. People can improve or get worse, depending upon what they do with what they have. The most advanced person is stable, like a mountain, and little things do not affect that person very much. The second personality type is described as being like a river; it is always moving and changing, but still it has its identity. The third is symbolized by a feather. It has an identity, but it goes here and it goes there, with each little change in the wind. It cannot stay long in one condition. Still, a person who is like a feather can become like a mountain, and a person who is like a mountain can become like a feather.

Perfection of mind is achieved in a Buddhist culture by practicing a Buddhist way of life. This way of life, called Buddhist dharma, can be applied at many levels. It can be simple or deep, differing in application according to a person's walk of life. Laypeople often follow a simple, essential Buddhist way of life; scholars may concern themselves with more complex intellectual aspects; hermits practice advanced methods of meditation; and so forth. No matter where you belong or what you do, you practice the teaching of the Buddha in the way best suited to you, and this establishes the best qualities. The teaching of the Buddha was originally a kind of guideline for how to lead a kingdom or a family, how to do business, how to live in a monastery, or how to do anything in a way that would bring the best conditions for all. This way of life might be called therapy today, and the religious masters who followed the pure teaching of the Buddha may be in some ways similar to therapists.

People do not necessarily need to be mentally ill in order to be out of balance and require therapy. Philosophical systems that limit a person's self-understanding can have powerful negative effects. When there is no understanding about mind, people can become completely identified with, and limited to, being Mr. or Mrs. such-and-such. To them, this flesh and bone body is all there is. Other people become identified with their image, and they are what they wear or what they do—as businessman, politician, soldier, teacher, and so forth. Those people who don't have an understanding of themselves beyond their body, their self-image, their name, their thoughts, will have a hard time when they begin to experience that they are more than these superficial appearances. To people who are open and mature, awareness of this deeper aspect of themselves can be very comforting, but for people who are not, it can be very difficult because it will create confusion for them.

The process of going more deeply into the mind produces side effects. One of these is that certain negative and positive emotions become vivid and exposed; you feel them more intensely, and they seem to become stronger. That is not really the case, though. Rather, your mind is becoming clearer so you are able to see things that were already there but obscured. It is like discovering an elephant in a jungle: at first you can't see it because of all the trees and vines, but when you cut down the jungle you can see the elephant plainly.

As perception clarifies, some people might even see and hear things that others do not. Certain types of people, whose subtle body systems are ultrasensitive, can become seriously disturbed by such phenomena if they are not able to under-stand and view them in the proper perspective. Other people, such as charlatans and fanatics, might waste a lot of time and energy on ego trips about such experiences, even to the point of damaging others. When something unusual happens it is best to just leave it alone and not make a big deal about it. Just leave it alone. These kinds of signs are not good and not bad. They mean that a process is going on, that's all. If you make something of those signs and amplify them, then it is almost guaranteed that something will go wrong that will take a long time to correct.

Such distractions come at the beginning stage of medita-tion, and if one continues in the right way, one will eventually experience the serenity of the meditative state. The method used to achieve this in Tibetan Buddhism is called *shinay*, or tranquillity meditation. Once one has learned to calm the mind, one can then enjoy the meditation itself, and everything will also remain clear after the meditation. It is a truly wonderful mental and physical feeling that is incomparable to anything else, but we should not become attached to it, because it is a stage in the development. It is the most perfect state of mind and body, and a powerful experience, and we cannot help liking it, but we must move on to the next step. If we become caught up in this initial stage we will be unable to progress. When we try to hold on to that particular good experience, it is quite possible that it will go away. If it does, we may feel like we are left with nothing and may give up further effort. Even if the state goes on and more unusual things are experienced, we will not experience the real, clear meditative state. If a person is deeply involved in meditation, not only as a therapy to calm the mind but as a Buddhist practice by means of which he or she is striving to achieve enlightenment, then there will be deeper levels of meditation and the experiences will be slightly different from those of a person who does meditation only for the purpose of calming the mind.

The difficulties that people face in their own lives or that they see being caused in other people's lives have sources and patterns of development that are explained comprehensively in Buddhist teachings. The basic ingredients for the conditions of suffering are attachment and anger, which come out of the foundation of ego, which is the sense of "I." Attachment and aggression are in everyone to some degree. There isn't any ordinary human being who is free of attachment and anger, though there is some kind of balance that can be kept. It is when this balance is lost that problems arise and people seek help through some kind of therapy or spirituality or both.

There are different reasons for going into therapy as well as different types of therapy. Physical therapy may treat a physical condition, such as after an injury or illness, but it can also be useful for improving conditions of the mind. Other types of therapy treat mental and emotional conditions. Body and mind are connected, of course; you cannot really separate them from each other. But there are differences in emphasis and aim, depending on the reasons and the kind of therapy a person is involved in.

Some people go to therapists because they have serious physical or mental problems, but many are neither physically nor mentally ill; they just wish to improve themselves as much as possible. Motivation is an important factor in therapy. Some motivation is deep, some is shallow. Superficial motivation, for example, might be involved when a person goes to a specially trained therapist in order to overcome blocks to communicating with other people. Some people might have difficulties in their family relations, and they go into therapy in order to gain some insight into their problems. If children have special difficulties at school they might be sent to an educational therapist. Each of these is a valid issue, involving a particular purpose; when that purpose has been fulfilled, the person may feel the job has been done. A deeper level of motivation brings people to therapy who have deep-seated emotional or mental problems. Therapy is a big issue for them because it has to do with their desire to have a meaningful life or one in which they can function normally.

There may be many different levels of need and motivation for obtaining help in the case of meditation, as well. It can be for body or mind, for superficial or profound purposes. The highest motivation, of course, is to achieve ultimate realization. One strives not only to develop good qualities in this life but to continue developing good qualities in the next life and many lives to come. The aim is enlightenment, which requires greater and greater clarity and realization, lifetime after lifetime. This is deep, vast, and limitless motivation. Most ordinary therapists do not treat their patients with anything beyond this lifetime in mind; their methods are aimed at alleviating specific problems in this life. Of course, if the methods used are effective for eliminating obscurations, the positive influences will extend to future lifetimes as well.

A therapist who follows Buddhist principles, though he may present them in a different context, will have similar results to those individuals who practiced these principles in the past. Whether it is called Buddhism or something else, the process will lead to ultimate awakening. For individual therapists to discover equivalent techniques on their own would be a difficult task. Life is short, and there isn't enough time for the necessary research and experimentation. A person who is not enlightened will make lots of mistakes along the way. That is the value of adopting a system that has been tried and tested by many experts over centuries.

Differences in achievement are caused by differences in method as well as in motivation. If you deal with attachment and anger at a superficial level, you may improve in a limited way, and you may solve some problems, but you will not become highly developed. If you deal with attachment and anger at a deeper level, a deeper development will take place.

Attachment is desire or longing for something; anger is having dislike or aversion toward the object. Anger can be so subtle you don't know it is there, or it can be very aggressive. Methods vary according to how subtle or gross the manifestations of attachment or anger are and how positive or negative they are. Meditation refines desire and anger, purifies them, and eliminates their most negative aspects in a gradual process. A high level of development may be reached in this way, despite the continuing presence of attachment and anger, which will remain to some extent, until all duality has been transcended and complete enlightenment attained. It is through attachment and anger that the development and one-pointed mental clarity of the human being are achieved. Each of the five poisons may be utilized in this way to bring a different aspect of mental clarity.

An ordinary human mind may attain clarity, which is free of confusion and distortion, without necessarily being enlightened. Such a person might not even be a first-level bodhisattva. He or she might be an ordinary human being whose mind is clear and sane. One develops this clarity of mind through meditation methods that are steps on the path of enlightenment. The clear-minded person is an effective and capable human being, able to see every situation clearly, without confusion. If, instead of just developing calmness and clarity of the mind, one looks deeper into the clarity itself and meditates on it, it will direct the way toward enlightenment. Reaching this clarity is an important step for a person who seeks enlightenment. If the motivation is to become a better human being, clear and not confused, the person will remain at the initial stage of calm, clear-mindedness. To reach enlightenment, something must be done to go beyond calm.

There are many meditation methods. Some are suitable for people who want to meditate to get rid of stress. Some methods involve physical or mental activities and speech. Others involve seeing, listening, and sitting. Some involve how and what you eat. Sometimes several activities are synchronized within one method. There is an appropriate meditation method for each situation; there is also a correct place for sitting meditation and a correct way to sit.

We don't really call vajrayana Buddhism therapy, although it does provide a way to work with imbalances that create psychological difficulties. There are a tremendous number of teachings and methods of this type in vajrayana Buddhism. What follows are examples of a few simple ones. Even the simplest methods require caution, however. If someone is not ready and practices incorrectly, they can go wrong. It is like using a sharp knife: it can cut things cleanly and easily, but if it slips and cuts your finger it can injure you very badly. Usually the people who go to therapists are very sensitive. They are like fully inflated balloons; if you touch one the wrong way it will burst. For these people the methods must be exactly right. They are affected by small things and become easily excited, depressed, or happy. This instability is the reason for being cautious. Physical, mental, or emotional imbalance from past experiences often creates this kind of instability. It is important for anyone wanting to practice these methods to first consult a qualified teacher or therapist knowledgeable in such methods.

Of the causes contributing to confusion of mind, the different types of emotions are primary. These emotions are generated from the five groups of defilements, to use Buddhist terminology: desire, anger, ignorance, jealousy, and pride. With undisciplined desire you become like a black hole in space—greedy, wanting everything. No matter how much you get, still you want more. When you are undisciplined in anger, the world becomes like hell, and you are unable to see whatever pleasant conditions are around you. You see everything as horrible and as a further reason for anger. When there is undisciplined jealousy, everyone's happiness becomes your suffering. Everyone's goodness becomes your problem. Undisciplined ignorance clouds perception so the mind becomes like an animal's mind; all you can think of are food and drink. Pride, when it is undisciplined, causes you to think so well of yourself that you feel you are the best, and you create situations for yourself in which you inevitably fall down. All of these have different ways of being played out, sometimes subtly, sometimes grossly, depending upon the causes and conditions in the individual's life. All defilements have equal power to distort reality. One is not worse than another. When any defilement gains control, it leaves a scar, which may be experienced as depression, confusion, or a neurotic pattern. This can range from mild to serious, as in the case of severe manic-depressive behavior and schizophrenia.

To avoid the confusion caused by these emotions, the first step is to discipline yourself so that your anger, desire, ignorance, jealousy, and pride will not have as much power over you. You should not allow these things to take over. But you cannot just discipline your mind on a superficial level; you have to go to the root and work from there. One way to accomplish this is to stop the supplies for the defilements, just as if you were fighting a war. When you don't let the opponents have water, food, or ammunition, they have to surrender. That is one reason why people sometimes make long- or short-term resolutions, called precepts, such as not to kill, lie, or steal. That is also why some people take ordination as monks or nuns, do retreats, or live a hermit's life of renunciation. These are all ways of diminishing the power of the five poisons. When you stop adding more wood, the fire naturally dies. These are specialized long-term practices that require clearly defined settings and life-styles. It is also possible to deal with each defilement directly, as it comes up, wherever you are. The following methods are traditional ways to deal with defilements. Again, it must be emphasized that these methods should not be practiced unless you are ready to do them, and this can be determined by asking the advice of someone you look to for spiritual guidance—a teacher with sufficient insight and knowledge.

Before beginning a specific exercise, certain preparation is necessary. You must set aside the time and have an appropriate place—a clean, quiet place where you will be undisturbed for half an hour or so. At the start of a session, sit for a few minutes to calm the mind. Sitting is very important because, when done correctly, it lines up the physical and mental systems so that you experience their connection and utilize that power in the best way possible. One can meditate in any position, but it is best to sit in a cross-legged position, on a cushion, with back and shoulders straight and eyes half-open. Relax in this position with everything as balanced as possible, for five minutes.

Once your mind has become quieter and your body more relaxed, focus awareness on your breathing by just being aware of it. Notice the four aspects of breathing: you breathe out, pause, breathe in, pause. Breathing affects one's physical and mental health. If the breathing is imbalanced, difficulties can result. For example, people who inhale and hold in the breath for a long period of time, exhale, and then immediately breathe in again tend to have hot-tempered, aggressive personalities; they tend to be angry most of the time. People who exhale and hold out the breath for long time, inhale, and then exhale immediately tend to have poor vitality. Making an effort to balance your breathing will help you have greater physical and mental balance. When you observe your breathing, breathe out slowly and completely, holding it out for two to five seconds; breathe in slowly and completely, holding it in for two to five seconds; and breathe out again. Do this naturally and easily. The breath should not be closed down or swallowed. It should not be rigid, but relaxed, with a natural rhythm. While breathing, rest the tip of the tongue on the roof of the mouth, just behind the teeth. Each round of breathing is one set, and you should do twenty-one sets to prepare yourself for the exercise.

The first method of working with the five major defilements is to let each defilement arise and then look at the nature of the defilement itself. For example, first think about something that you are really attached to, letting your desire become really alive; then stop the development of the desire and look at the state of desire itself. As you do this you will see that the desire is not there. It is not a solid thing, but a built-up illusion. Then do the same thing with anger; think of something that makes you angry and when the anger is intensified, just look at it. Again observe the illusory nature of the anger. Next build up ignorance. If there is a particular thing about which you have more ignorance than you would like to have, or something you are not able to understand, use that. Intensify the quality of ignorance and then leave it alone and just look at it. After that, do the same thing with jealousy, then pride. When you develop pride your ego will feel full, complete; just let it be. When you look into the ego itself, it will naturally become nothing.

This practice is called the self-liberation of the five defilements, because it is through the characteristic of each defilement itself that the defilement is liberated. Although it is a very effective method, care must be taken; developing defilements in this way might create difficulties if you are not ready and just let the defilement take over. You should first be competent in directing your thoughts and disciplined in dealing with your defilements. You can go through the exercise several times. After you complete your session just sit for a few minutes. Do another twenty-one sets of breathing and sit for another five minutes before getting involved again in your daily activities.

Often, meditators do not re-enter their activities peacefully and comfortably after meditation. It is common for people to do their meditation session at a particular time and find a particular routine for it. If they are doing something when that time comes they drop everything to meditate, and when they finish meditation they rush off to what they were doing before; this makes the meditation session as neurotic as anything else they do. It is good for the practitioner to develop calmness in doing things. It is an illusion to think that by going about things hectically you can get more done. You can get more things done with less hurry if your mind is clear. You can use the time, rather than letting the time use you.

The next meditation method is for people who are extremely attached to their bodies. This technique is good for certain people, but not for everyone. For some people it might be harmful. If you are strong and mature enough to handle it, and if it is appropriate for you, it is a very effective practice. If you decide to try it, begin as before, with the sitting and breathing exercises. Then focus your attention in the center of the forehead. Move with awareness through the skin, muscle, and bone, looking into these parts of the body from inside. Move your focus of attention slowly down through your body. Let your attention move through your arms and hands, into your heart, down to your navel, and so forth, until you reach the bottom of the feet. Notice what is there as you go through; honestly look at everything you have, seeing the whole body as it is: outside, inside, deeply inside. After expanding your awareness and seeing clearly what is there, focus again in the center of the forehead, and sit in that experience for a while. Conclude the session with sitting and breathing exercises. This technique will help you to overcome the illusion of the attractiveness and permanence of the physical body. The purpose is not to make you neglect or hate your body, but to help you develop an appreciation of its true substance. Seeing the body's impermanence, you will tend to take better care of it; you will also become less attached to it because you will understand how vulnerable it is.

The next two methods are similar in structure, though they are done for different purposes; the first is for depression and the second is for manic behavior. These practices, which involve visualization, color, and breathing, are simple but can be very effective. Again, care must be taken: first consult with a teacher or therapist.

Begin with the routine of sitting and twenty-one rounds of breathing as before. After the five-minute rest period, cleanse your breathing, exhaling forcefully through the nose three times. Keep your hands on your knees while sitting in the cross-legged position; each time you breathe out forcefully, also stretch your fingers as far as you can. Inhale moderately fast, completely, and hold the breath in one or two seconds. Then breathe out with force, as completely as you can. Do this round of breathing three times. Keep your body as straight as possible. Now you are ready to begin the visualization that counteracts depression. Visualize a long tube extending from a place beneath the navel to the crown of the head, where it has a big opening, like the mouth of a trumpet. It is white in color, very straight, and the top is open. It is composed of solid light. Don't think about anything that is in the body. Experience this channel of light just as it is, as being like emptiness. While you visualize this, at the center of the chest visualize a white four-petal lotus. This white lotus is facing up, and in the middle there is a ball of light that is like a white pearl, about the size of a pea. It is energetic and light, so it sits just above the lotus, ready to go. It does not sit heavily in the lotus. Until that visualization is clear, just breathe normally, not thinking about your breathing. The sequence in the visualization is to first visualize the channel from the bottom to the top, then the lotus in it, then the ball of light. Keep the whole thing in mind, focusing more on the ball of light. When that is clear, breathe slowly and completely, holding the breath in maybe one or two seconds, and then breathe out forcefully and completely. As you breathe out, send this white ball up through your crown opening as far as it will go. It stays there until you breathe in. As you breathe in slowly and completely, the ball comes down and settles on the lotus again. Do this a few times, depending on how you feel. For some people doing it many times is good. When it stays up it becomes the highest and brightest thing in your awareness. At the end, dissolve the tube first, then the lotus, then after that the ball. You don't have to work hard at it; just dissolve it and it disappears. Cleanse your breath again three times and conclude the session as usual.

The technique for wild, manic behavior is similar but uses the opposite color and direction. The channel is visualized upside down. The lotus is black, resting upside down in the center of the chest. In the center of the lotus there is a black ball of light, with a color like the best quality of black pearl. It is very heavy, ready to fall down. The black lotus holds it like a magnet. As you breathe out, the black ball falls down. Let it go down as far as possible through the earth, straight through. When the exhalation is complete, hold the breath for a few seconds so the black ball stays below you, and at that time you may have a sense of real groundedness, of being heavy, inside the earth and grounded there. As you breathe in, the black ball of light comes up. It is pulled back up to the lotus and it stays there. This visualization can be difficult for some people, who find that going down is easy, but coming back up is hard to do. It does not matter if you cannot perceive the ball coming up as described; it will come slowly up and sit there on its own. Do it several times, and afterward dissolve it as before: first the channel, then the lotus, and then the ball, one after another. Cleanse the breath again three times, and conclude as usual.

Finally, the following method works at a higher level of mind, similar to some advanced meditation techniques, though not quite the same. Begin with the preparatory breathing, as before. This time, after the five-minute rest develop your devotion and compassion to its highest level. Do this by thinking with devotion of those who are more spiritually advanced than you, and with compassion for those who are not. When this feeling reaches the greatest intensity, stop the effort of developing it further and just remain in the full feeling of devotion and the pure feeling of compassion. Let all the sentimental aspects of devotion and compassion dissolve layer by layer, like the skin of an onion. Each layer brings you a little bit deeper. For beginners, devotion and compassion are pure sentiment, but as one practices, the sentimental aspects dissolve and genuine devotion and compassion remain in a state of authentic purity. There is no way to describe it exactly; it must be experienced.

The practice of these vajrayana methods requires appropriate preparation and conditions. Exactly how you should do a particular technique, when you should do it, and your own individual emphasis while doing it should all be determined by a qualified teacher. This is necessary for it to be an effective, positive, and beneficial experience for development. If techniques are irresponsibly applied, without full knowledge and experience of the consequences, greater mental distress, instead of healing, can result. Vajrayana meditation practices, however simple they may appear, are far-reaching in their effects on body, speech, and mind. Just as a doctor who prescribes powerful medicines must be qualified, so must the spiritual guide who employs meditation therapeutically.

Healing is a natural part of a daily life that is in mental and physical balance. The state of good health in this case is a result of applying instinctive wisdom. Natural healing is not necessarily something that happens after damage has been done, but something that does not allow the damage to occur.

Even if there has been damage, there is a kind of alchemy in nature that can turn damage into a healthy growing process. The growth process can be a therapy in itself, leading to new areas of understanding and new abilities. Everyone has the potential for achieving all the possibilities of the perfect human being. Through the growth process a person develops or liberates that potential, just like a seed that germinates. If a person does not grow, that potential becomes distorted or wasted. In childhood, adolescence, and adulthood—in each step of life—one has to cross a threshold. If there is not healthy growth and development, these stages become disordered, and a person ends up pretending he has grown into the next stage when he has not. If he has not really crossed that threshold but pretends that he has, then one way or another he will eventually have to face that reality. Usually people are not willing to face it, and because of this all kinds of problems come into their lives. Recognizing and acknowledging where one is and working with whatever situation life presents—accepting it just as it—is an important step toward mental and spiritual maturity.

When a person is healthy on the mental level, the next step is to go beyond this dualistic balance toward higher realization. Before a person can even think about doing this, however, basic mental harmony must be attained. Any type of mental imbalance also has a physical correspondence; therefore the physical balance must be corrected and healed. Daily habits have to be improved and regulated so that they contribute to both physical and mental harmony. In this approach there is an element of prevention, which is rooted in discipline. Proper discipline prevents physical disharmony. When the discipline of beneficial daily habits permits physical harmony, then mental harmony is encouraged and maintained.

It is through the mind in the relative world that we attain realization of our ultimate nature. We must care for the mind just as we care for the body, giving it nourishment and exercise designed to sharpen its abilities and maintain healthy tone. Healthy tone of the mind is clarity. It is through the window of clarity that we can see the ultimate and become conscious of the reality of our own ultimate mind.

Part Two

SOUND

4
LANGUAGE

*Symbols of sound
help dispel ignorance.*

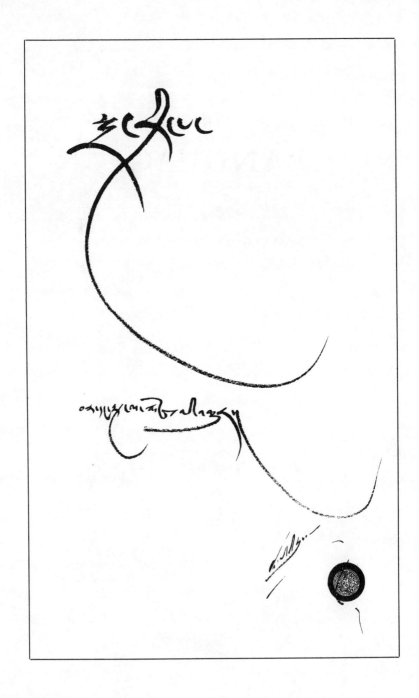

L ONG AGO HUMANS USED THEIR INTELLIGENCE to begin organizing sound into language, with which ideas, feelings, and information could be communicated in specific ways. Language developed from simple grunts into words, alphabets, large vocabularies, organized sentences, and rules of grammar. Modern languages enable us to communicate with accuracy and with beauty.

Communication methods are one important aspect of sound and expression, but in the Tibetan Buddhist tradition the study of sound includes a great deal more. Beginning with basic verbal and written communication skills, this body of knowledge progresses to the specialized arts of poetry, music, and performance, as well as astrology and related sciences. It includes subjects that might be found in the humanities and fine arts divisions of a university today. Sound is also the basis of mathematical science in this system.

The initial areas of study might be loosely grouped together under the heading of language. In the Buddhist context, this study is concerned with an in-depth examination of the fundamentals of grammar and the development of terminology and names of things. The goal of the study of language is to communicate in such a way that the meaning is clear, whether it is in an ordinary letter, a serious literary work, or a spoken presentation.

A knowledge of grammar introduces the possibility of a more sophisticated way to communicate. A particular meaning can be expressed efficiently and accurately, in a way that would not otherwise be possible. Grammar is a key to what lies behind communication.

The Tibetan alphabet of thirty letters was adapted from the Sanskrit alphabet, although the structure of the language itself does not much resemble Sanskrit. Tibetan is considered part of the Tibeto-Burmese family of languages. A scholar by the name of Thönmi Sambhota was sent by the Buddhist king Songtsen Gampo to India to study language and to create a written alphabet and rules of grammar so that the Sanskrit texts on Buddhism could be translated and preserved in Tibetan. In the monosyllabic language that has developed, words are formed by adding prefix and suffix letters to a root letter. The letters have gender depending on their function—as root letter, prefix, or suffix—and the gender must be in agreement. There are several genders, which could be translated as masculine, feminine, neuter, super-feminine, barren-feminine, and genderless—the last being slightly weaker in pronunciation than the neuter. Generally, the root letter is the first letter that is pronounced and the one that carries the vowels and other specialized characters. There are five vowels, including *ah,* which is a sound inherent in every letter. Specific rules govern the interaction of these letters, but basically the strong go with strong to emphasize strength, the weak go with the weak to emphasize weakness, and mediators between strong and weak create harmony; without these mediators there would be conflict. Masculine combines with masculine, feminine, or neuter; feminine with feminine, super-feminine, or neuter; neuter never combines with itself.

There are eight categories that in English would be called cases, beginning with nominative and followed by seven others that indicate direction, action, possession, location, and so forth. Certain additional letters or words—particles—indicate each case. There are other particles that are used with verbs to indicate past, present, or future tenses of regular and irregular verbs, or for negation. Tibetan also has a large vocabulary of honorific verbs and nouns, which are used in polite conversation, whenever one is speaking to someone respectfully. The common words are used when speaking of oneself, close familiars, or those in a lesser position, such as children. There are also Sanskritized letters and words that are used in sacred texts but not generally in the day-to-day language. This is a brief outline of the structure of Tibetan grammar, which provides the basis for the development of the language into its scholarly and artistic forms.

Higher levels of language are used for philosophical discussion, teaching, prayer, and in tantric Buddhist mantras. The purpose of prayer or mantra is to affect the individual through the purity and sacredness of the words themselves. These special words are thought to be blessed by the saintly people who wrote the prayers and also by the many people who recited them in the past with devotion and clarity of mind. Anybody who recites these particular words or phrases somehow feels the meaning of the words directly. Recitation of sacred words reserved for times of prayer and meditation is connected to the inspiration and transmission that is an important part of tantric Buddhism. The mantras are especially significant because they are said to contain great power to directly link the individual's physical existence, the mind, and the universe. These words can have a profound effect if the secret of their power is transmitted and understood correctly. Mantra is a high point in language, where the relative world can express the ultimate mind in an extraordinary way.

A most important aspect of language in the Tibetan Buddhist system is *ngönjö*, which might be translated as "the study of names." *Ngön* means "not hidden," a kind of exposed clarity; *jö* means "to say." This science of names includes a depth and impeccability that is not really indicated by the English word *name*—which by definition is an organized sound, a word by which something is known or described. There are what might be called first-generation names, second-generation names, and so on. A first-generation name is the first simple name that is given, such as "stone," "tree," or "sky." There is no way to know how such a name came to be given, except where there are histories of the meaning and origin. The origin of words forms a separate science similar to what is known as etymology in linguistics. In a second-generation name, knowledge about its origin is evident in the way it is used, as in "heart of stone." And there are words and word combinations with still more elaborately developed expressions of meaning.

Any simple word can have numerous names that express the meaning on different levels, ranging from the ordinary to the scholarly to the highly poetic. An example from Tibetan is the moon, *dawa,* which is a first-generation, simple name. A second-generation name for moon is "the lord of the night"; another is "that which has the cooling light," in contrast to the sun, *nyima,* which is "that which has the warming light." The moon is also "the reflection of the sun." These are the sort of complex names that are specifically used in poetry, to make the language aesthetic as well as accurate. Even ordinary literary works or speeches require more than one name to describe thoughts and to do a thorough job of communicating, with all the nuances of feeling, attitude, atmosphere, and specificity that the writer or speaker wishes to convey.

Many of the texts for the study of names are comparable to thesauruses, in that they give numerous terms to describe each simple word. There are other texts that deal with style. For example, style in an original work differs from that in a work of commentary. The Kangyur is the Tibetan title for the collection of sutras, or discourses of the Buddha to his disciples, which are considered the actual words of the Buddha. The style in the books of the Kangyur differs from that in the Tengyur, which is the collection of commentaries upon the original sutras.

This example of the direct words of the Buddha, which comes from the *Punyabala-avadaana-sutra* in the Kangyur, is on the subject of generosity.

Gifts should not be given with carelessness or greed,
Nor out of desire for merit.

In order to benefit, one
Must give with awareness and wisdom.[1]

Another example from the Kangyur is the following teaching given to Lord Brahma, at his request:

"Brahma, whatever you desire, request to the Tathagata, because of your request itself I will make your mind content." And then because the Buddha was open and presented the opportunity to Brahma, owner of the immeasurable universe, Brahma supplicated the Buddha by saying: "Bhagavat, Tathagata, Great Compassionate One, greatest of all the great bodhisattvas, what is it that quickly brings perfect enlightenment, by what amount of completion of perfect qualities is enlightenment attained?" As requested, Lord Buddha pronounced this to Brahma, lord of the immeasurable universe: "Brahma, the greatest bodhisattvas of all great bodhisattvas, if they have completely perfected one quality, they will quickly complete and develop the most pure and comprehensive realization."[2]

Another teaching based upon a request—a common formula in the sutras—is one given to an old village lady who asked where death, old age, life, and skandhas[3] come from. The Buddha replied:

Sister, birth does not come from anywhere; old age does not come from anywhere. It doesn't go anywhere. Sickness does not come from anywhere; it also doesn't go anywhere. Sister, form does not come from anywhere, feeling and perception and all the impulses and consciousness do not come from anywhere, and do not go anywhere.

This repetitive type of delivery is also typical of this style. The Buddha goes on to explain:

Sister, it is like this: the wood useful for kindling a spark, together with the effort of human beings, creates fire. That fire will also burn grasses and trees, but without such causes, it will die.[4]

The following excerpts from the Kangyur are of an altogether different kind of writing. These are examples of tantric writing of a mystical nature. The passages are made deliberately obscure and use a special vocabulary, called "vajra language" (*dorje tsig*). To understand them properly the instruction of a qualified teacher is necessary.

Vajra dakini, the great bliss, greatest joy seen by the eye, and so forth, are empty, therefore the nature of all these is emptiness. Seen without thought, that will become unobstructed. This is the nature of space. Everything is the nature of space, mind. Having meditated without obstruction, freedom of thought will be fully born. The Bhagavat, glorious Vajrasattva, the Tathagata pronounces this.[5]

A one-line chapter from the same book is even more symbolic in its style of language:

Other points I will teach also, so the six dakas may be understood fully. When united with the six dakinis, all the power points of the body have one syllable upon them. The first is at the chest itself, the second is at the head, the third should be given to the crown and the fourth is at the armoured shoulder. Eyes are the fifth; the sixth is mentioned for everything. From the great vajra dakini, this is the fourth chapter.

An example of instruction for practice is the following "moon and sun profound instruction":

Right and left in combination move according to the natural order. The left channel starts from the roof of the mouth, entering the center of the body to the area of the navel. In the moon channel facing downward, the vowels of the moon always flow purely. The right channel continues from the navel, entering the roof of the mouth. In the sun channel facing upward, the consonants of the sun always flow from the two doors of the nose. Characteristic of the flow of the two channels is that left is the path of entering, right is the path of going. From the rising sun until the sunset is the day. From the sunset until the dawn is the night. Day and night are divided.[6]

The use of such unconventional symbolic language is considered the most direct and nondualistic mode of expression. The examples give an idea of why it is necessary to have an unbroken lineage of transmission of the meaning of such passages.

The Vinaya, the body of teaching on discipline for monks and nuns, contains advice on how to keep the various commitments. The following shloka is from the *Vinaya-karika* in the Tengyur and is about the nature of theft.

Using others' clothing as if given,
Using medicines or spells to get what you want,
Choosing the best when there is a selection,
Taking what is not given, even to give to another, becomes
    theft.[7]

Following are two other examples of advice to monks, specifically, the rules for novice monks. The first discusses the vow not to kill.

For one who is mentally normal, having taken the novice
    vow,
If he deliberately kills another human, with full knowledge
    and effort
Unless the victim does not die or it was in a dream
The vow of the person who kills will be destroyed.[8]

The second discusses intoxicants.

> Of liquor created from fruit and so forth,
> Wine of grapes, alcohol from sugar cane, or distilled from
> mashed grains,
> Of these causes of intoxication,
> Not even so much as a drop on a blade of grass should be
> taken.[9]

The following example is from the Abhidharma and is part of the commentary on the words of the Buddha. The subject is awareness.

> Whoever takes joy in quietness, be it day or night,
> The disciple of Gautama
> Will pleasantly wake
> To be awakened.[10]

A different style of writing is found in the following commentary on attachment and craving.

> Craving is the chief cause of samsara. Absence of craving is craving which is abandoned. Craving is absent because you abandon all instinct of craving, also because abandoning this is the abandoning of the foundations of the bonds of samsara. It is said if possessing is abandoned, that is the absence of craving. The circumstance that creates possession is craving, but there is nothing in samsara to take but attachment, morality, view, sacrifice and self.[11]

This excerpt is about the path.

> The last stage means an end of samsara. Knowing it correctly means to understand it not wrongly. This level of understanding will reveal nirvana with traces of skandhas. Following this, by knowing the ultimate, one will be liberated at the end of all existences. Without knowing the ultimate, one will not be

liberated. This is the definition of reaching the end of existence. The liberation with no trace of skandha is the reaching the other side, because by means of this one crosses the ocean of samsara, which encompasses all dualistic existence.[12]

Another example comes from a specific kind of tantric text called a dharani, which consists of long mantras with brief commentaries on their uses.

Rain falls,
The running mountain water
Washes surface refuse away, just like this mantra.
Whoever sees it or chants it,
Their defilements will be purified.[13]

It is, perhaps, a little difficult to observe in translated pieces, but the style of the sutras is much more straightforward and authoritative than that of the commentaries.

Strict rules govern the use of language in every situation. The mature writer, after years of studying and memorizing grammar texts as a student, continues to use them for reference and as tools for perfecting the art of language. The basic grammar texts are those composed by Thönmi Sambhota— the *Sumchupa* and the *Tagjukpa*—and the *Situ Sumtak,* which is a commentary written by Situ Chökyi Jungne.

Through the highly structured systems of knowledge that include grammar, terminology, and poetry, the student can not only discover the relationship between the relative truth of language and the ultimate truth of sound, but also benefit others through the gift of clear communication. By impeccable use of the rules of language, the master will gain greater realization personally and also communicate and stimulate such realization in others. Language becomes an important discipline when its link to the body-speech-mind interrelationship is considered. It is one way to bring the three together harmoniously and to use that expression for the benefit of all those one contacts. It is not only necessary for poetry or scholasticism but for daily expressions of kindness and concern, where language can become a vehicle for our growing compassion and wisdom.

5
POETRY

Beauty of word
is ornament of meaning.

KNOWLEDGE OF NAMES IS ESSENTIAL IN the specialized study and art of poetry. Descriptive names are chosen for their beauty and mood to blend with other poetic components and to harmonize with the sound as it is being used to express an idea.

When a poem is written, the accuracy of meaning and sound must be synchronized. It should not be rough but smooth, unbroken by conflicting sound. Two opposite sounds cannot be spoken fluently and beautifully together. To combine them would make an unpleasant experience out of something that is meant to give pleasure and inspiration. Of course, the poet might deliberately try to make it unpleasant, but that is not usually done in the Tibetan school of poetry, where there are elegant ways to express even unpleasant states of mind, such as sadness or anger. The perfect poem naturally and spontaneously synchronizes sound and meaning as it is read. This harmony of sound begins with the fundamental agreement between letters which, as outlined in the previous chapter, is the basis of grammar. Poetry builds upon this.

Poetry, generally speaking, consists of the main subject, the ornamentation of the subject, the orientation of the subject, and the action of the subject. The subject itself is like a person at the beginning of its life. That person is born into the world naked. A name is then given to that bare form, and it is dressed, groomed, ornamented, and enriched through different kinds of learning. Eventually this stylish and educated person must do something; otherwise all that preparation would be wasted. The person has a certain orientation which determines his or her approach to work, to study, and to the world in general, and which gives the individual motivation. Each life has a unique purpose. Poetry is like that.

The adornment of a plain idea must be accurate and in line with the point that the poet wishes to express. The poet must develop expertise in describing the subject without ornament as well as in using full ornamentation. Whether concerned with details of color, mood, or action, the poet must be able to write fluidly. The method of learning how to do this is to become familiar with the rules of poetry and to then apply them over and over again.

There are many kinds of poems—from the simplest description to ornate and highly symbolic styles. The rules of poetry define how poems can be written using many different perspectives, attitudes, and means of description. These conventions can then be improvised upon. To describe a parrot very simply, for the purpose of definition and without ornamentation, you might say that the beak is red and curved, the wings are green and flexible, the throat has three stripes, and

Puzzle poem: "May the roots of all goodness, / Loving kindness and compassion, / Grow in the pure heart soil / Of all sentient beings, now and always."

The four-line poem in the grid may be read horizontally, vertically, backwards, and forwards, and is an example of one of the poetic skills developed in the Tibetan tradition.

it makes a loud noise. In this case you would not say that the parrot possesses a beak of coral and wings of jade, that it wears three ruby rings around its neck and converses sweetly. This would be an ornamental description.

A poet might choose to focus on description of action alone:

When the noise of thunder announces drizzling rain,
The peacock's cry lifts to the horizon.
People of the village run out to the field,
Gather their dry clothes and bring them home.

Here there is no definition; there is only action. The purpose is to express that action. A poet can also express qualities. Take the Buddha's qualities, for instance:

Nothing limits ability
His attainment is ultimate attainment
His realization will never fade
His understanding is beyond finality.

Important in poetry is the aesthetic mood, an ancient refinement of expression which is derived from Sanskrit texts on the subject. Mood applies to all types of art, but particularly those involving sound. The Tibetan system lists eight moods, or "tastes": heroic, wrathful, humorous, sad, frightening, loathsome, peaceful, and glorious. The fundamental activities of the great universal forces provide the material for poetic treatment. It is the infinite play of creation—unfoldment, enrichment, destruction, and absorption—that inspires poets everywhere.

While learning the art of poetry the student writes poems according to each of the several hundred rules of poetry. Each rule has subcategories which might be called characteristics. The following poems are written according to the conventions prescribed in the texts. It is by writing poems in this way that the student learns all the methods of classical expression.

The first poem is written according to the second characteristic of the twelfth rule, *raptok*, which means "complete understanding." Whatever subject is chosen, it must be one that is thoroughly understood, because the poet is required to make every possible assertion in order to make it clear, dramatic, and aesthetically pleasing. Ten to twenty poems are written in order to demonstrate a thorough knowledge of the subject. The following poem on the subject of Tara is written from the standpoint of "mindless" raptok—mindless in the sense of not being related to mind but to things of nature; only natural things are used to make the point. Tara is the great female bodhisattva who embodies the female aspect of compassion. She is one of the most popular deities in Tibet, and her image appears everywhere in temples and homes.

Her exquisitely wide seven eyes
Are challenged by the flower above her ear.
It appears that all of Tara's seven eyes
Are envious of the utpala flower.[1]

The next poem follows the thirteenth rule, which has sixteen combinations of characteristics. This poem is from the point of view of cause, the fifteenth characteristic. The poem asserts a basically incorrect premise, which might also be taken as correct if viewed from a perspective that differs from the usual one.

Your powerful intelligence, learned one,
When the 100,000 suns of its brilliance are displayed
Makes the lotus of ignorant minds
Seem to close completely.

The following poem is written according to the fourth characteristic of the first rule, *yonten rangshin jöpa*, which is straightforward, with no dressing. It is a poem about fear.

Fire in the stainless sky,
The phurba of Vajrakilaya.[2]
When evil ones just think of it
Weapons fall from their hands.

The next poem has a twist; something is described through evoking its seeming opposite—in this case, feminine qualities are used to enhance the description of a great warrior. This poem is an example of *pegyen*, "example adornment."

Unsurpassable, universal hero,
At the moment you confront your mighty opponent
You are graceful as a loving maiden;
Your bow sings like the tamboura of the goddess.[3]

The following poem is according to *rangshin jöpa* and represents the fourth subsidiary rule, *dze*, which has to do with the description of attributes. This poem is about Manjushri, the bodhisattva of wisdom and knowledge. Deities in Tibetan iconography often have identifying attributes and paraphernalia. Manjushri's main attributes are a book of knowledge surmounted by an upright, fiery sword on his right. The form of Manjushri described below is the four-armed Manjushri, who carries a bow in his left hand.

A sword to cut doubt from its roots
Held over numberless volumes of teaching.
One who possesses the bow and arrow tames the ego of the
    Four Maras.[4]
Bestow auspicious opportunity, O highest Lord of Wisdom.

The next poem is again from *pegyen*, "example adorn-ment," the sixteenth subsidiary rule, which has to do with poems written with inappropriate comparisons. "Lord of Seven Horses" is one of the descriptive names for the sun.

The Lord of Seven Horses is bright, but he is not liberation.
The strongest hero can be defeated in the battle of
    defilements.
The Lord of Liberation who holds the lineage of saints
Has no object of comparison.

Next is a poem based upon deliberate mixing of images—in this case, male and female. It is from pegyen, the fourth characteristic of the second subsidiary rule, which deals with juxtaposition. The inspiration comes from the Hindu epic *Ramayana*, in which Rama is the hero. The expression "per-fect brows" is a poetic term that describes the beauty of a goddess.

The brightness of the face of Perfect Brows
Dazzles the thousand eyes of the God King.
The smile of her sidelong glance
Is like the arrow of Rama.

The next two poems are according to *jarwa*, or "glue together," the fifth rule. Poems written with this rule in mind combine symbolic elements in a particular way, utilizing various meanings of a single word to create a multi-level image. The first poem is about samsara, the self-perpetuating cycle of existence. In it, the flute is characterized both as an instrument and as a symbol of the seeming substantiality and endlessness of samsara:

The gloriously gentle flute plays a variety of illusory
    melodies.
When its virtuosity is heard

It deceives even the strongest of minds.
Why eternalize the play of the worldliness game?

The last poem is also written according to the fifth rule, but
demonstrates a slightly different angle: the nondiffering result
of two different manifestations of phenomena. This poem is
also about the deceptive nature of samsara.

The foundation of impermanence and change,
The object of illusion of all beings,
A smiling, fully bloomed lotus,
Along with worldly pleasure, deceives.

Such poetry comes from hard work and the experience of
composing many different types of poems. Some very complex forms of poetry resemble puzzles and require much skill
and concentration to create. In one particularly interesting
type, the poem is written in the form of a diagram, on a grid;
the poem may be read in any direction—forward or back-
ward, up or down—without losing its meaning. Poetry is not
something one dreams up suddenly, without discipline, when
there is nothing better to do. It is a serious undertaking.
There are about 280 axioms in the primary text on poetry,
but these represent only the fundamentals. The second rule
alone has thirty-two major combinations, four secondary
combinations, and sixty-five particular examples, all of which
must be learned and applied.

Through training the student develops an ability to express
exactly what is meant to be expressed—no more, no less. A
good poetry teacher will tell the beginning student that poetry
is in everything; it has no beginning or end, it is limitless, and
the only reason for learning and following the rules is to
develop the ability to explore that limitlessness. The rules are
guideposts that give the poet an idea of what poetry is about,
but the end is to know and appreciate the poetry in all

manifestations of the universe and to then express it spontaneously. Someone once asked why it is necessary to learn 280
axioms in order to be spontaneous; the answer is because we
are not spontaneous. When rules are learned and one becomes expert in applying them, then genuine poetry can be
written freely and spontaneously. The true poet will never go
against the rules because he or she cannot go against them;
they are part of a poet's nature. It is like learning to walk on
different kinds of terrain: once you know how to do it, you
do it automatically, jumping from rock to rock without a
thought and without tripping up. Poetry is body, speech, and
mind interacting with the universe. It is relative world playing
with ultimate mind.

6

PERFORMANCE

*Skill of mind and body
manifests miracles of sound and form.*

THE BRANCH OF KNOWLEDGE THAT combines sound with movement is performance. In Tibetan it is called *dögar, dö* meaning both "to sing" and "to repeat" and *gar* meaning "physical movement." Performance can involve verbal expression, gestures, dance, and music. The purpose of performance is to convey an idea by using the physical modes of expression: voice and the movements of the body.

Performance can be based on an original work or an ancient work, or it can be a spontaneous expression that follows the rules of the art. The special quality of performance is that it can communicate much in a short time—the significant events of a lifetime or of a period of history. It is not limited to life stories or legends, however, or to any particular span of time. It can describe a thousand years or the events of an afternoon. It can also deal with imaginary situations that could not occur in real life. Mundane events, fantasies, and profound truths are all possible subjects in the performing arts.

The Mahakala dance is an example of performance that is practiced in monasteries in connection with a ritual prayer ceremony, or puja. As sacred dance it is a separate study from the lay performances, though many of the principles are the same. The Mahakala dance is performed for several purposes, the first being meditation. The dancer meditates according to the Mahakala puja as it is described in the liturgy and performs a particular part of the puja as he dances. The Mahakala dance is always performed by monks.

Mahakala is the wrathful embodiment of compassion. The purpose of doing any Mahakala prayer ceremony is to overcome defilements and negativity in a most powerful way.

Those in the audience who know the prayers and are advanced practitioners participate mentally along with the dancer, who is literally performing the practice through the art of gesture, dance, and chanting. Those lay people who are unable to follow the rite participate by receiving the blessing of the puja, which assists them in overcoming their obstacles. By participating with the right attitude, even though they are unable to perform the meditation, they receive the protection of Mahakala. This type of religious rite also blesses the environment, turning it into the mandala of the protector Mahakala. The term *mandala* is used to describe the protected, purified space of Mahakala. The dance defines this space vividly for the participants and audience.

Sacred dance requires a great deal of preparation. The head dance master is usually someone who has spent his life perfecting his art. It takes years for a dancer to become proficient. The monks who perform must learn the pattern of movement and gesture, which must be synchronized with the other aspects of the puja in progress: the music, chanting, the meaning of text, and the visualization. The dancers closely follow the text of the Mahakala puja, which is derived from the tantra, the texts on practice. The dance steps and gestures have evolved in a particular way in each of the great monasteries that practice the Mahakala tantra, with each monastery having its own tradition of interpretation. Costumes are also designed according to the descriptions in the texts and traditional Tibetan iconography. The colors and types of brocade robes; the hand-made masks of protectors, animals, and other figures visualized in the puja; and the symbolic paraphernalia used in the dance are not haphazard but come from an ancient religious and artistic tradition.

The pattern of steps in each dance and the sequence of dances conform to the arrangement outlined in the text. The first dance blesses the ground in preparation and invokes the Great Protector. It is performed by the champön, the dance master, who is dressed in the "black hat" costume of a tantric.

The next dance dramatizes the coming of Mahakala and retinue and welcomes the deity. Here the figures representing Mahakala, Mahakali, and the minor protectors and animals in the retinue emerge in colorful masks and brocades. After that is a dance depicting Mahakala vanquishing negativity. The obstacles are represented by a small effigy that the dancers symbolically destroy using ritual implements that signify the particular weapons attributed to Mahakala. After overcoming the defilements the visualization is dispersed into emptiness. The next dance is an offering of gratitude to the protectors, and the concluding dance is one of praise and glorification of Mahakala. Other dances depicting the Masters of the Cremation Ground, the deities of the four directions, the deer and other sacred animals, or the protectors are often included in the program. Although the presentation often varies according to the custom of the particular monastery, the basic liturgy remains the same.

Sacred dance functions on many levels at once. It uses the movement, music, color, time, and space to act out a drama on the physical level, while at the same time including a profound and subtle mind practice. Sacred dance is another method of unifying body, speech, and mind to express and experience ultimate truth. The coordination of mind training, or meditation, with the physical world is the essence of this practice.

Secular performance is also valuable; it affects people in different ways, depending on the kind of music and performance. In Tibet and Bhutan laypeople often perform secular dances with themes that are related to Buddhist stories and are sometimes similar to the themes of monastic dances. Others are based upon the epic of Ling Gesar, the legendary king whose miraculous exploits are the subject of many Tibetan songs.

Several conditions must be present in order for a performing artist to become a skilled master. Just as in other fields of knowledge, excellence in performance requires effort and talent. Even though everyone possesses the potential to manifest any skill, because of causes and conditions, as well as the limitations of one lifetime, some of an individual's abilities are more easily developed than others. If a person has physical grace, a talent for mime, dance or singing, chances are that great skill can be developed in the performing arts. The length of time it will take depends on natural ability, the difficulty of the subject being studied, and the knowledge of the teacher. The best way to make the most of an ability is to work under an experienced master. Through a master who has assimilated wisdom from hundreds of great artists of the past, a student is given the opportunity to get the most out of his or her effort. There is less chance of wasting time. In monasteries the senior dance master is often a very old man who has been dancing and studying dance traditions since he was a young boy. He has probably trained students for most of his life. The dance master at Palpung Monastery is around eighty years old and still quite agile. Such venerable holders of dance lineages are highly respected in the monastic community, because they are a rich resource of traditional art.

Music, which also falls within the subject of performance, has long been developed as a way to achieve, experience, and transmit perfect sound. Such development has occurred most notably in India, where the Sanskrit texts on the subject, which were later translated into Tibetan, originated. An illustration of the power and refinement that sound in performance can reach is a story from the time of the Mughal emperor Akbar about the legendary musician Tan Sen. First it must be remembered that in music, as in all other aspects of knowledge, the elements and their interplay are very important, and much consideration is given to the time of day, season, and so on that correspond to these elements. There are ancient ragas, or melodies, that evoke these elemental qualities and are reserved for special times.

Once Tan Sen was called by Akbar to demonstrate his mastery of music to the court. In preparation, unlighted lamps were placed around the hall and the master was asked to play a *raga dipaka,* or "lamp melody," which expresses the fire element. This he did so skillfully that all the lamps were lighted by his art, and the story goes that as he continued to play the heat began to burn him, also. It was only by calling in his wife, also an adept musician, who sang a monsoon raga that sucessfully brought the rain, that Tan Sen was saved. This story demonstrates the level at which a master can command the elements and express perfect sound in performance.

In India music has long been used to induce certain feeling states, those same moods that are expressed in poetry. The advanced purpose of music is to beneficially affect both physical and mental levels through sound. A perfect sound can generate a perfect atmosphere. In that perfect atmosphere a perfect moment can manifest that can be either profoundly meaningful or ordinary, depending on the depth of the individual and the depth of the music itself. Every sound creates an environment and affects everyone in that environment in some way.

Music is a universal language, and it can communicate to all living beings at many levels simultaneously, to the point at which it connects the relative world with the ultimate mind. The accomplished musician has the capacity to express whatever is suitable to the moment, so that the music has the intended, powerful effect. Anyone who listens to music in the West or in the East, particularly when a great artist is performing, can experience that something special is going on there. Even when certain talented musicians perform music that is ordinary, the sound itself can influence moods dramatically. From this ordinary experience it is possible to have a glimpse of music's deeper potential. We can imagine the impact if what we consider to be perfect sound were refined several times, or a hundred times.

Sound is appropriately joined to movement in the art of performance, because every sound is produced through movement and sound itself is an expression of movement. Drama and dance can have great effect on the audience when performed with perfection. This art of performance is not confined to the stage or to television. It is a fact that a person's every action throughout life is also performance. All of the small things we do are interrelated with everyone and everything else in one great performance. Through creative involvement in daily life, we all have the opportunity and the ability to develop skill in performance. By refining our words, our gestures, our actions—all of the ways that we shape our environment and the atmosphere in which we live—we can develop impeccable performance in our lives. It is possible in this way for us to become masters of our lives and for our lives to become masterpieces.

7
ASTROLOGY
AND GEOMANCY

*The actuality of interdependence
is rarely seen, but accuracy
develops understanding.*

ANOTHER BRANCH OF KNOWLEDGE THAT falls within the study of sound and expression is known broadly as astrology but includes within it mathematics and the science of geomancy. These are practical sciences that utilize the elements and laws of nature to explain circumstances of life so that one can find the best way to adapt to these circumstances and derive benefit from them. Knowledge of these sciences can help in situations that affect both physical and mental conditions.

ASTROLOGY

The fundamental principle of astrology is that the smallest thing in the universe goes through the same processes as the largest; the same rules apply to both, and in fact an action in one sphere reflects an action in the other. What affects us in our daily life reflects what is also affecting the universe. In the relative world we observe that something minute, such as a seed, can develop into something large, like a redwood tree. We see that short can develop into tall, or a child into an adult. Science has shown that all of the instructions for the fully developed human being are imprinted within the cell at conception. In the ultimate mind, however, there is no small or large, developed or undeveloped, even though, paradoxically, each small thing affects the universe. This significant piece of knowledge can be applied in many different circumstances once it is understood.

Mathematics also holds a key to the secret of all living beings because through mathematics the workings of the universe can be traced. Mathematics is the foundation of both astrology and geomancy. It is so advanced a science that if one had the knowledge of mathematics, the time, and the motivation, one could take a current event and trace back, through all of the interrelated causes and conditions that led up to the event, to the beginning of time. Future events, causes, and conditions could also be determined by using mathematics to trace from the present moment to infinity. In Buddhism this interplay of causes, conditions, and events is called *karma* in Sanskrit. Karma is what results from the actions of an individual, and while these results may sometimes be felt in the same lifetime, often they manifest as causes and conditions in later lifetimes. Beneficial actions create auspicious causes and conditions, or "good karma," such as good health, wealth, and so forth; harmful actions create negative causes and conditions, or "bad karma," such as disease and other difficulties.

Mathematical calculation and the principle of the small reflecting the large are the keys to understanding time and matter in the science of astrology. Time and matter are interdependent. Time includes past, present, and future. Matter includes the elements and the directions, which are associated with space, also considered an element. Astrology uses calculations to make correlations from which the specific cause, result, and condition of any situation can be determined because it is related to a larger, nonspecific cause, result, and condition. In this way the fate of a person, a country, or the world can be learned.

There is an old story of an astrologer who was calculating his own chart when he saw, to his surprise, that it indicated that his death would occur at any minute. He was in good health and thought he must have made a mistake. He was cleaning his ear with a metal toothpick, thinking he would do the calculation again, when some boys threw a ball that came through the window and hit his arm, so that the metal pin was driven into his brain and he died. Stories like this are told to emphasize how accurate astrology can be.

It is important to grasp the meaning of fate in Buddhist

astrology. Fate is a process and not an end in itself. That is why fate is variable. Fate is also the reason something happens; it is connected to the causes and conditions that produce a natural result. Taken in the right sense, fate is when everything happens at exactly the right time for something to be accomplished; nothing happens until the right causes and conditions are present to allow it to happen. If you strike a match, you may find that it is damp and will not ignite. There is nothing hopeless about such a situation: it is dependent on causes and conditions, a function of relative truth in the relative world. If you have the appropriate knowledge you can work with these circumstances to bring about a more satisfactory result. At the same time that causes and conditions create a certain result, it is also true that anything can happen and that there is no fixed limitation. There is a limitless variety of causes and conditions, and anything can happen any time and any place within the framework of these changing circumstances.

It can be useful to know about the converging causes and conditions that indicate fate, because often, when these are known, something can be done to counterbalance the negative forces that result in difficulties. Since causes and conditions are created by our own actions, we can also create positive causes and conditions by offering prayers or performing beneficial works, such as saving sentient beings from harm or death, giving to the poor or ill, and so forth. If we are faced with a situation that cannot be influenced and must be accepted, then knowing about it and the reasons for it can assist in bringing about understanding and equanimity, and bringing us closer to true balance and realization.

In Tibetan astrology each year has twelve months, which are called "homes of the sun." The year is seen as being like a horizon, in the center of which is Mount Meru.[1] The sun revolves over Mount Meru, and it stays within a particular area, or "home," for one month. The fifth month brings the sun above the mountain's peak, so that the days are long. In the ninth month the sun is farther from the mountain and lower down, so that the days are short. Each year does not necessarily begin in the same "home of the sun." Which zodiac sign comes first is determined by calculating when a particular star returns to its original position after 365 days. Unlike the Western calendar, the Tibetan calendar's twelve-month year consists of 360 days. Instead of having a leap year, in the Tibetan system an extra month is inserted every few years—at a point indicated by astrological calculations—to make up the difference. That extra month will become a duplicate month of one of the twelve, rather than being tacked on at the beginning or end. There might be two tenth months, for instance, or two fourth months, depending on the results of the calculations.

Six of the months are male and six are female. Each month has a characteristic that is exemplified by a symbol which in most cases is similar to those of the Western zodiac. Beginning with the first month, the symbols are: the vase, fish, sheep, ox, man and woman, crab, lion, girl, scales, scorpion, bow and arrow, and lord of the sea, a kind of sea-monster. There is also a twelve-year cycle in which each year bears an influence characterized by one of the following: tiger, dragon, horse, monkey, dog, mouse, rabbit, snake, sheep, bird, pig, and ox. These animals are also applied to each of the months as subattributes. The twelve-year cycle is extended into a sixty-year cycle when the animals are joined with a particular element and gender.

The days of the week are also under the influence of the sun and planets. The assignment of planets to days of the week are the same as those in the Western system of astrology. In the Tibetan system the days are named for the planets rather than gods: the sun, *za nyima*, the moon, *za dawa*, Mars, called *za mig mar* or "red eye," and so forth. Tibetan astrologers, like their Chinese counterparts, give importance to the position of certain stars, in addition to the position of the closest planets, when drawing up charts and making interpretations.

The interaction of the elements is taken very much into account in all astrological determinations and calculations, and to this end each element is assigned a numerical value. Calculations of which times are auspicious and which are dangerous for undertakings can be precise down to the day and minute. The relative auspiciousness of days or years is calculated from nine *mewa,* or numerological factors, each of which is assigned a number, element and color.

1	white	*metal/iron*
2	black	*water*
3	blue	*water*
4	green	*wood*
5	yellow	*earth*
6	white	*metal/iron*
7	red	*fire*
8	white	*metal/iron*
9	red	*fire*

The mewa are recorded on a rectangular grid, their positions determined by calculations. The changing positions of the mewa on the grid reflect the various influences coming together in positive and negative ways. "Black" years, considered inauspicious, occur when these influences join forces to become malefic, which happens only in the years of the snake, tiger, monkey, and pig, and only when the number two mewa falls in the center of the grid when calculating the influences for that year. The way in which the mewa are used to predict negative or positive trends in an individual's life, based upon the date of birth, is reminiscent of the biorhythm system that has gained popularity in the West.

The four directions are also described according to their elements and zodiacal affinities. Each of the cardinal directions has two parts, upper and lower. For the east, the upper is tiger, the lower is rabbit; its nature is wood. In the south, the upper is snake, the lower is horse; its nature is fire. In the west, the upper is monkey, the lower is bird; its nature is metal/iron. For the north, the upper is pig, the lower is mouse; its nature is water. The southeast is dragon, its nature is earth; southwest is sheep, its nature is earth; northwest is dog, its nature is earth; northeast is bull, its nature is earth. This information is also utilized in determining which days are auspicious or inauspicious for activities.

One simple way of viewing the philosophy behind astrology is through understanding the influence of the basic elements of nature. This is only one aspect of astrology, and many other factors are involved, but this description gives a partial idea of how astrology works. For instance, the most agreeable combinations of elements are thought to be earth and earth, water and water, and earth and water. In the texts it says that when earth is together with earth there will be extra stability. If we start something at a time when earth and earth are together, then what we manage to accomplish will be done without obstacle. It does not necessarily mean that everything will get done, but it is a good indication that what is done will be stable. It is a particularly good time for building houses or anything that must last for a long time. Another good combination is water and water. When water and water come together they blend into each other harmoniously. That kind of contact or connection creates unity and inseparability; it is beneficial for strength and dignity, and for avoiding disharmony. For a doctor, it is a good time for making medicine. It is also beneficial to hold marriage ceremonies on days when water and water come together. The third good relationship is earth and water, because these elements help each other. When water comes to earth, it is absorbed into earth and gives it strength. When water and earth are together, happiness will remain. This combination indicates a good time for creativity, like making clothing, or for having any kind of festival or celebration.

Next are the three stable relationships: fire and fire, air and air, and fire and air. In the texts it says that fire and fire together doubles strength. If one fire reaches five feet in height and another is added, the two fires can reach ten feet. It is said that on a double fire day whatever you try to accomplish you will succeed. It is a very good time for starting a business or charitable work, especially ventures that might be difficult to accomplish. Another stable combination is air and air together; the texts say that this builds strength, in the same way that a hurricane develops when air from different directions meets and combines forces. Air and air together signifies speed and is a good indication for things that must be done immediately or with great speed. It is also good for traveling—you can start out on that sort of day, or you can start with that kind of person as your companion. And it is good for breeding livestock. A double air day is the perfect time for a nomad to bring his animals together. The last of the stable combinations is fire and air. The text says that fire and air together develop strength. It is as if a lion and a tiger become friends; they form a powerful friendship, full of strength. It is an auspicious combination which can influence things to happen, just like that. It could be called a lucky combination: it is not necessarily practical but can bring an unexpected good outcome. This is a good time for doing something that requires power. It is a good situation to start with—a spark for your enterprise.

Lastly are the three negative combinations: fire and water, earth and wind, and water and air. The most unfavorable of these is fire and water, which are in opposition and which counteract each other. The text says that the combination of fire and water is death. It is a good indication only for a negative undertaking, like making war, perhaps. Earth and air are not total opposites, but they do not work well with each other. There is no area where they complement each other. When earth and wind combine, things become very dusty and unpleasant. The influence of this combination, then, is wastefulness. If a business or any other endeavor is begun under this influence it will go badly. If it is a business of buying and selling, chances are that the maximum will be spent and the minimum earned. Nor is it a good time for building or buying a new home. Another unsuitable combination is water and air. Again, these elements do not work together or complement each other. It is quite bad for friendship and invites slander, deception, and so on. If that kind of negative activity is desired, then beginning on a day when water and air are together will be very successful; otherwise it should be avoided. The last negative combination is earth and fire. Of this combination the texts say it burns destructively, it creates stress, pressure, and suffering. It is therefore a bad combination for making friends, developing friendship, doing anything that involves cooperation between people.

The relationship between elements can also be symbolized as mother, son, friend, or enemy. For instance, iron "uses" wood, as in the case of an ax-handle, and wood is therefore a friend of metal; however, since iron destroys wood, it is wood's enemy. Water "uses" fire for heat, though it also extinguishes fire, so fire is a friend of water, but water is the enemy of fire, and so forth.

TABLE 1
Elemental Relationships

Mother of water is metal	Friend of wood is earth
Mother of metal is earth	Friend of earth is water
Mother of earth is fire	Friend of water is fire
Mother of fire is wood	Friend of fire is metal
Mother of wood is water	Friend of metal is wood
Son of wood is fire	Enemy of wood is metal/iron
Son of fire is earth	Enemy of metal is fire
Son of earth is metal	Enemy of fire is water
Son of metal is water	Enemy of water is earth
Son of water is wood	Enemy of earth is wood

Tibetan astrology also makes use of the system described in the *I Ching*, which in English is usually known as the *Book of Changes*, while in Tibetan it is called *Parkha*, derived from the Chinese *Pakua*. This system consists of eight trigrams that represent the elements, the directions, the seasons, and the fundamental universal forces. They are depicted in the Tibetan system, as in the Chinese system, as combinations of unbroken and broken lines, which signify the two basic dualistic forces of the relative world: creative, strong, masculine principle (yang) combines with the receptive, yielding, feminine principle (yin) to create the infinite phenomena of the relative universe. The wisdom and means of yang and the compassion of yin unite to produce manifestations that are just one step from total realization and at the same time very ordinary. These principles do not fight each other, because even though they appear to be in opposition they are actually

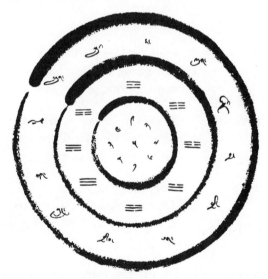

This astrology chart depicts the tools of the astrologer in their appropriate positions: the *lokar*, or cycle of twelve years represented by animals; the *parka*, or hexigrams symbolizing the elements and their interplay; and the nine *mewa*, important numerological factors used in exact, day-to-day calculation.

complementary; they are unified, just as light and dark, two manifestations of these principles, are inseparable and define each other. The trigrams describe the relative world—its laws and its changing cycles of harmony and disharmony. They reflect the order of nature; the effects of wind, water, fire, and earth; and the seasonal changes. All these principles also have applications at other levels and are indications of more profound truths.

TABLE 2
Examples of PAKUA, or I CHING, Trigrams

Trigram		Associated Symbols, Qualities, and Directions
☰	Creative	Heaven, strength, sun, horse, wisdom, knowledge, head, father, jade, metal, cold, hardness, fruit from trees, deep red, northwest.
☷	Receptive	Earth, yielding, devotion, compassion, shade, cow, softness, tranquillity, belly, mother, cloth, yellow, southwest.
☳	Thunder	Movement, arousing, dragon, spreading out, eldest son, decisiveness, forcefulness, dark yellow, spring, east.
☴	Wind	Penetrating, gentleness, wood, eldest daughter, guideline, work, long, high, advance and retreat, indecision, white, southeast.
☵	Water	Danger, pig, ears, ditches, ambush, bending and straightening out, melancholy, sad hearts, blood, moon, red, winter, north.

☶ *Mountain*   Keeping still, resting, dog, hand, fingers, third son, standstill, bypath, little stones, doors and openings, fruits and seeds, northeast.

☲ *Fire*   Light-giving, dependence, sun, lightning, pheasant, tortoise, crab, snail, mussel, eye, middle daughter, coat of mail, helmet, weapon, dryness, summer, south.

☱ *Lake*   Joy, pleasure, sheep, mouth and tongue, youngest daughter, sorceress, smashing and breaking apart, concubine, autumn, west.

Though the trigrams in the Tibetan system are similar in meaning to those in the Chinese system, the Tibetans utilize the *Parkha* mostly in astrological determinations that are arrived at by mathematical calculations, as well as in geomancy; the *Parkha* is not commonly used in Tibet for divination using sticks or coins, as has been popular in China. In Tibet, each day of the year is assigned its *Parkha* symbol. Every person has a particular trigram that influences them, according to their day of birth. The trigrams are used to forecast auspicious or inauspicious days. For instance, a day that corresponds to the creative trigram is considered good for planting trees, laying the foundation of a house, or ornamenting something, while a day under the influence of the receptive trigram is not good for building a foundation, though it is good for planting trees or fencing in land. Days for making ritual offerings are also determined by the *Parkha*. A water trigram day is good for making offerings to water deities or doing practices that bring rain or hailstorms, but it is not good for digging wells or canals. A day upon which the wind trigram falls is good for recitation of mantras, whereas a day of the mountain trigram is not. Much of this may seem arbitrary; such a system is hard to understand without a knowledge of the subtle interactions of the elements, and the natural and social phenomena that are symbolized by each of the trigrams.

Besides mathematical calculations, an examination of a person's physical features, personality, health, facial expression, tone of voice, hands, and living environment enable a competent astrologer to understand the fate of that individual. If the physical surroundings of a house are examined—taking into consideration the exact location of the house, the date of construction, and other major features—a great deal can be told about the occupants' history as well as their fate. This is not a simple science, and it takes exhaustive study and considerable expertise before the advanced stages of understanding can be reached. Through calculations and observations both abstract and concrete, a master of this knowledge can determine anything that one might wish to know. He is able to understand and recognize the causes and conditions, the results and reactions, of the universe—from the most ordinary level to the most cosmic.

GEOMANCY

Geomancy is an English term for an ancient science of environmental design based on the flow of energy. In Chinese this art is known as *feng-shui*; in Tibetan it is *sache*, "earth observation." Of the many possible ways to fulfill the physical and psychological requirements of life—such as comfort and convenience, clarity, tranquillity, and confidence—one important way is to adjust our surroundings. The art of geomancy helps to do this by removing environmental circumstances that hinder peace of mind and body and creating those that are conducive to it. Good soil, water, and a favorable climate will enable a seed to grow into a strong tree or a delicate flower, but if one of these factors is missing or insufficient, growth will be hindered. In the same way, people are influenced by the surroundings and atmosphere they live in. These environmental factors can determine how people progress.

The most vast and all-pervading environment is the universe itself. The environment that seems closer because it is more available to our ordinary perceptions is our corner of the world, which includes mountains, rivers, plains, roads, buildings, and other features inseparably connected with the four directions. Wherever we happen to be located in this environment is the center for us. Our neighborhood is our home, and the most immediate environment is one's body.

We are affected by where our home is, how it is built, which rooms are occupied, and which are reserved for what activities. All the things people do can be divided into the two categories of activity and rest. When you are active you direct energy outward, and when you rest you are subjective and focusing inward. When you are active you are less vulnerable than when you rest. You are the most vulnerable when you are sleeping; someone can more easily attack you or take advantage of you when you are sleeping than when you are awake and alert. In addition to the actions of others directed toward you, subtle forms of energy also affect you: planetary energy, thought and emotional energy from those around you, and energy currents from the world and the universe. If you live near a factory or a nuclear power plant, you will be affected by the energy it generates in the environment, just as you would be affected, in a different way, if you lived near a forest or a clear mountain stream. When you are active, subtle energy affects you less than when you are resting, and especially less than when you are sleeping. It is due to these continual currents of energy that the location of one's house is important to consider.

Your surroundings should be chosen according to these energy currents, and the most favorable sites are those that receive and make the most of the beneficial energies available. The location of your house can affect your health, emotions, personality, finances, and family relations either beneficially or adversely, depending upon whether the surroundings are harmonious or discordant in terms of energy flow. It can affect how you do things and how you live your life.

If you think back on your life, on the times when you lived in different places, you might observe how various things happened to you as a result of your surroundings. You might even be aware that certain locations seemed to be better for you than others. Life's influences have many facets, and cause and effect operate in simple yet deep ways, permeating everything. The science of geomancy is a study of the effects of environmental energies, the operating principles of these energies, and the steps that can be taken to improve circumstances by harmonizing environmental forces and incorporating the environment's inconspicuous forces into architectural and landscape design.

Just as geomancy affects an individual situation, it also influences nations. Geomancy is reflected in a country's history—the rise and decline of civilizations, the length of their existence, wars, and other significant developments. A person knowledgeable in geomancy can examine the geography of a place and, without having a familiarity with the country otherwise, tell a great deal about the past, present, and future prospects of the people living there. Geomancy is a method of discovering why things happen to a person or a nation, and it also shows how an unfortunate situation might be remedied for the good of all.

The Mahabodhi Stupa in Bodhgaya is an example of a well-placed monument. Hills encircle Bodhgaya for hundreds of kilometers. Bodhgaya is located in the central area, in a hole, which creates a pool of energy, and the Mahabodhi Stupa is built in the middle of that pool. There is an entrance from the east, and the bodhi tree is in the west; the stupa is in the middle of this well-balanced environment. This sort of environment indicates that though there will be ups and downs in Bodhgaya's situation, it always will remain important. For example, the bodhi tree was attacked many times, but part of the tree continued to grow, even after deliberate attempts to destroy it. The site of the stupa is considered a very stable and powerful spot—stable in the sense that it is not vulnerable and exposed—so it will survive for a long time.

The Potala Palace in Lhasa, Tibet, is another example of powerful geomancy. The Potala is considered to be in the middle of a lotus, with the surrounding mountains being like petals. The little hill in the middle of the valley, upon which the Potala is built, is like the core of the lotus. The building itself is very well balanced. It faces directly to the south, which is the most tranquil direction to face since it is least affected by astrological influences. The palace is also protected as the core of a lotus is protected by its petals. Because the Potala is the largest building of the entire Lhasa area, and all the buildings in front—for the officials, shops, and houses—are lower, it has the strength of a palace that rules, a palace where the ruler lives and functions. All of these factors insure that the Potala will be very well known and have tremendous influence, though it, too, will have many ups and downs. To function, it is necessary that the person who lives in the Potala be very powerful, with tremendous energy and special qualities; otherwise the person will not be able to survive.

The Forbidden City in Beijing is one of the most perfect examples of geomancy. When you look at a model or plan of it you see that everything is balanced, in harmony, and interconnected. The complex faces south, and all the important buildings are in the center. The entire complex is surrounded by water, which keeps the energy inside; water flows from south to west and from east to west, all the way around, so that on the west side the complex is entirely protected by water. The most important part of the complex is the center of the main building, the Hall of Supreme Harmony, which is low like a pool. Behind it is a mountain range, which covers the north side. The south side is much more open. The site of the Forbidden City is central to the natural features that surround it for hundreds of kilometers. It is in harmony with the mountain ranges, the flow of the river, and the flow of the wind. The complex itself has been aligned and built according to the most sophisticated and advanced geomancy principles, and it will last for many, many years as an important building, despite ups and downs. When it comes to feng-shui, there is no ultimate place. Every place has its time. The longest time mentioned is 360 years. The durability of a building, depending on the strength of its location, can be 60 years or 12 years, but the Forbidden City is definitely a 360-year place.

Mastery of the arts of astrology, mathematics, and geomancy can be valuable not only for the practitioner but for the many people whom the master advises. A negative situation can be transformed into a constructive one. Realization is more easily attained when obstacles have been identified and removed or made harmless by emphasizing the beneficial environmental influences. Mathematics, astrology, and geomancy take on obvious importance as helps along the way for the individual who is striving to integrate relative and ultimate realities while progressing toward realization.

Part Three

INNER
KNOWLEDGE

8

SCIENCE
OF TRUTH

*The two truths can clarify
assertion and denial.*

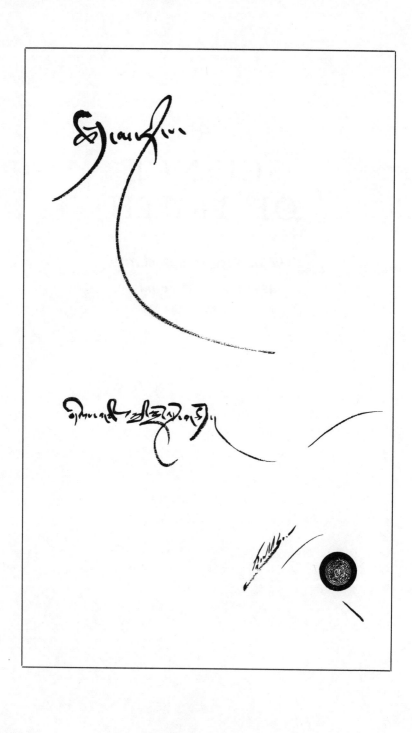

THERE IS A TYPE OF KNOWLEDGE THAT, when applied, can overcome wrong view and misunderstanding. It deals with a specialized area of truth. The Tibetan word *tsema* describes a method of proving the validity of something by making true and correct assertions about it. Through this process the most comprehensive definition may be arrived at, regardless of the subject. Because of the precision and means involved, *tsema* is usually translated as "logic," the closest English equivalent for this science of truth.

Anything can be explained according to either a correct view or an erroneous view. The erroneous view may seem very plausible. To be completely sure of correctness, the accuracy of the explanation must be tested. The correct explanation will be accurate and the wrong one will be inadequate. The reason for going to so much trouble is that whatever is practiced with wrong understanding will have an imperfect and possibly harmful result, while whatever is practiced with right understanding will have a beneficial result. Naturally we would like the best results. Individuals can be easily and innocently misled; therefore it is necessary to build a structure that will allow an individual to avoid harmful views and help to develop a correct understanding. This method might even be called advanced common sense, because it is like common sense, though not quite as simple. It is a development of common sense that eliminates distortions of truth that can arise as a result of our lack of perfect awareness and understanding. If the technique is learned thoroughly, there is less chance of making errors in judgment than with ordinary common sense.

A major principle that runs through the study of logic is

the awareness of relative truth and ultimate truth. Relative truth relates to the time and condition in which we as individuals find ourselves—our relative world. The relative principle allows an individual to relate to the variables of the situation, but it is all the while backed up by ultimate truth and ultimate reality, which allows us to avoid getting carried away by changeable interrelationships. The ability to balance between relative and ultimate is a significant part of the development of logical truth. When these principles are firmly established in one's awareness, then others can be taken up for study and application, such as cause, condition, result, and interrelationships. As a student masters each principle in turn, his or her means of relating to every situation becomes the most appropriate means because through study and living what is studied one gains clarity and a deep understanding that is founded on a sound knowledge of logical truth. When this kind of insight is achieved it can be used to correctly interpret any type of situation.

The method begins with a subject. The subject must be precisely formulated or the discussion would at best be a useless diffusion of energy. This subject is then defined by describing it according to its qualities and attributes. Fire can be said to be fire because it produces heat, because there is flame, because it burns, because of a characteristic color and shape, and because it produces smoke. The opposite kind of definition must also be formulated. If there is smoke, there is fire; or if something glows, burns, or is hot, there is fire. Then the reverse is stated. If there is not fire, there will be no smoke, no heat, no flame, and so on. This is an elementary example of how truth is tested by means of logic.

The two arguments that follow give an idea of how a debate might be carried on. An actual debate, of course, is often quite specialized, focusing on fine points and references to famous arguments of the past that have been studied by the debators. The debate follows a prescribed form, which includes gestures and characteristic words and phrases that make up traditional expression. The following arguments are highly simplified and are only meant to give a general idea of what takes place.

Relative Truth and Ultimate Truth

Position 1: Relative truth and absolute truth do not conflict.

Position 2: Relative truth and ultimate truth conflict because they are two separate truths.

Position 1: Relative truth is the law of cause and result, which creates the outer manifestation of everything, and ultimate truth is the essential inner nature of this manifestation, so they are parts of the same truth and not in conflict.

Position 2: That makes two interdependent truths. If truth is interdependent then it cannot be the truth. Interdependence makes it incomplete in itself because it is dependent upon something else for its existence; therefore it cannot be the truth. And if both truths are equally true, how can they not conflict?

Position 1: They do not conflict because ultimate truth is the ultimate truth of the relative world, and relative truth is the relative manifestation of the ultimate nature of all things. Ultimate truth and relative truth are both equally valid because they are the two aspects of the truth. Without realization, however, any presentation of relative and ultimate truth can only be relatively true.

Emptiness

Position 1: Everything is emptiness.

Position 2: Everything has true existence.

Position 1: Everything is empty because phenomena are the products of changeable, illusory conditions and therefore are illusion.

Position 2: Everything is solid and has true existence because it is there and we perceive and experience it. If you are hungry and you eat, you feel full. If somebody is shot with an arrow through the heart, the person dies. This is real, not illusory.

Position 1: Because everything is empty, you can have an empty stomach; because everything is empty you can eat food and feel full. Everything is empty, therefore you have a body and an arrow can kill it. Because everything is empty, endless phenomena can manifest.

Position 2: That is not so. If everything is empty there is no arrow and food cannot fill you. If everything is empty then an arrow cannot kill you.

Position 1: On the contrary, because of emptiness the arrow can manifest as a production of all its conditions. All the particulars of space, atoms, time, and so forth—the phenomena that manifest within their own conditions, like the arrow—manifest endlessly because of emptiness. Because of emptiness, karma, cause, and conditions manifest as the body; when the stomach and food come together, you feel full; when the arrow and your body come together, you die. Everything is empty because all of this can happen, and all of this can happen because everything is empty. If it were not empty, if the true existence of everything were not empty, none of phenomenal reality could manifest as it does. The argument that everything has true existence, eternalistically, is invalid because everything is impermanent and subject to change; everything is a manifestation of all its conditions, and the conditions themselves are also manifestations of their own conditions. Everything is emptiness.

Typical examples of classical debate are those that took place between early schools of Buddhist thought, which challenged some of the tenets of Buddhism. Each school held a slightly different theory; these differences became the subject of elaborate dissertations. Three such schools of thought are the Vaibashika, Sautrantika, and Chittamatrin, which arose about 150 B.C.E., three hundred or so years after the parinirvana[1] of the Buddha. The Vaibashikas did not accept that the mind could be aware of itself and an external object at the same time, and they asserted that external objects have true existence. The Sautrantikas accepted self-consciousness as well as the existence of external objects. The Chittamatrins did not accept that external objects truly exist, but they did accept the true existence of phenomena dependent on causes and conditions. The debate between proponents of these three schools, which went on for years, is a famous example of a controversy regarding the nature of matter and time.

The Vaibashika and Sautrantika schools held that ultimate reality consists of the smallest, indivisible particles of matter and the shortest, indivisible moments of time. Relative reality was held to be complex combinations of these ultimate components, resulting from causes and conditions, that is, karma. The Chittamatrins rejected this idea, holding to the view that only mind exists.

For a moment to be the minimum increment, it would have to be indivisible, all three schools maintained. The Chittamatrins refuted the theory of the Vaibashikas and Sautrantikas by maintaining that for such minimum units of time to link up to form linear time, they would have to be composed of a beginning, by which they linked to the previous moment, and an end which led to the next moment. Without these linking factors the indivisible moments would have the value of zero, and no amount of them could form a length of time. The Chittamatrins held that the very notion of a "smallest unit of time" having a beginning and an end invalidated the claim of its indivisibility, because a moment could then be separated into parts.

In the same way, the Chittamatrins held that it would be impossible for the smallest particles to be indivisible. If these particles linked with other particles to create a mass of matter, they too would require facets which would allow them to link with other particles. Without these facets, the smallest, indivisible particles would also be of zero value, and they would be incapable of attaching themselves to each other to create form. If it is accepted that a particle of matter has the top, bottom, and sides necessary to link, the smallest particle becomes divisible and the theory of indivisible particles is invalidated by the same argument that invalidated the theory of indivisible moments. Such arguments went back and forth, in great detail, between the schools of thought. This is only one brief example of a classical philosophical debate that falls within the scope of the science of truth.

There are many stories in the texts about contests between famous teachers who met in debate. One is about a learned monk from India—Shantarakshita, whom the Tibetans called Khenpo Bodhisato, or "Bodhisattva Abbot." Shantarakshita lived during the time of King Trisong Detsen, and he was one of the three main persons of the time who contributed to establishing Buddhism in Tibet, the other two being Guru Padmasambhava and King Trisong Detsen himself. Shantarakshita was a famous logician who had been invited to Tibet by the king. He remained there for many years, helping to set up a college at the monastery of Samye. He taught that the accumulation of merit and wisdom was a step-by-step process that required study, application of Buddhist principles, and meditation. A school of those who practiced his teachings sprang up in Tibet.

After Shantarakshita passed away, a Chinese monk called Hashang Mahayana came to Tibet and taught that only one path and one single practice was necessary for enlightenment, and that a step-by-step process was not necessary. His idea was that one should stop both positive and negative thinking, since both a white cloud and a black cloud obscure the light of the sun. His theory concluded that to reach enlightenment one had to stop all thoughts. Those who took up his philosophy became fanatical about it. The application of his theory made people very rigid, since they were not supposed to think, and mental disorders often resulted. This, along with the fanaticism, began to have negative effects on the development of Tibetan Buddhism. The disciples of Shantarakshita were disturbed by this state of affairs, and they recalled that before their teacher had passed away he had prophesied that an obstacle to the lineage may arise; he had advised that if this happened, a disciple of his in India named Kamalashila should be invited, and that he could help overcome the obstacle. The king of Tibet was a devout Buddhist who respected every Buddhist monk, so he also had great respect for Hashang. He hoped the problem would be settled in a dignified way in a debate. So the king and the disciples of Shantarakshita invited Kamalashila to Tibet to give assistance in this matter. When the delegation of people who were sent to invite Kamalashila arrived, he responded to their invitation by saying that if the teachers who were the opponents were intelligent, learned, and good in logic, then he would be able to clarify the error, but if they were not intelligent, if they were ignorant, then he would not be able to help. Kamalashila wanted to set up a test to find out.

Kamalashila went into Tibet as far as the Tsangpo River, which was on the way to Lhasa, where it had been arranged that he would meet Hashang. Hashang was waiting, standing on the other side of the river. Kamalashila, who was walking with a stick, spun his walking stick three times above his head and then put it down on the ground. By doing so he posed his question to Hashang, which was, "What is the cause of the three realms of desire, form, and formlessness?" Hashang was wearing a Chinese robe with long sleeves. After the question had been posed, he pulled his hands inside the sleeves and held his hands up above his head, with the long sleeves drooping over them, so they could be seen by Kamalashila across the river. This was his reply, and it meant that the three realms were caused and created by subject and object, or dualism. Because his hands were hidden inside the sleeves, they symbolized the ignorance that was the foundation of subject-object duality.

When Kamalashila saw this, he was convinced that he could

123

help the disciples of his guru, Shantarakshita, so he continued on to Lhasa, until he came to the king's palace. At the request of the king and the disciples of Shantarakshita, the two monks prepared for debate. Hashang sat on one side of the hall and Kamalashila sat on the other. The king of Tibet presented each of them with a beautiful flower garland and said, "I am a layman, and I cannot judge either one of you, so whoever is convinced of the other's philosophy and thinks the other has mastered him, then I request that person to give the garland to the victor. I will request the one who gives up his garland to leave Tibet, and he will be given every courtesy." In this way the king avoided expelling any venerable monks and was able to maintain proper forms of respect for whoever was proven to have the faulty view. Kamalashila and Hashang sat face to face and debated.

Kamalashila's point was that the accumulation of merit is necessary in order to have accumulation of wisdom, and to achieve this the practice of overcoming negative thought by positive thought and positive thought through realization is necessary. He maintained that stopping thought, whether it positive or negative, is not based on a correct view. His arguments and proofs were so astute that Hashang conceded his position. He surrendered his garland to Kamalashila and returned to China, and the lineage of Shantarakshita continued to flourish in Tibet.

Two other masters who were very important in the spread of Buddhism in Tibet, and well known for their scholarly abilities, were Atisha Dipankara from India and Lotsawa Rinchen Sangpo from Tibet. In the mid-ninth century King Langdarma had tried to wipe out Buddhism, and in the years following his reign the teachings became distorted due to a lack of knowledgeable Buddhist teachers. Yeshe Ö, ruler of the kingdom of Guge in Western Tibet had sent Lotsawa Rinchen Sangpo, among others, to study in India with Buddhist masters so that they might bring back to Tibet a pure lineage of Buddhism. Yeshe Ö and some of his family were devout Buddhists, and many times they invited Atisha, who was probably the most renowned teacher in India, to Western Tibet. Atisha had taught at the great universities of Bodhgaya, Odantapuri, and Vikramashila. He finally visited Tibet, coming to the region of Ngari, where he met Lotsawa Rinchen Sangpo in approximately 1040.

Atisha tried to find out what teachings were needed and why he had been invited all the way from India. He asked Rinchen Sangpo what he had learned. Rinchen Sangpo, who was much older than Atisha, replied by enumerating the sutras and tantras he had studied, and when he had finished Atisha said, "There was no need for me to travel here from India when there is already such a learned person as yourself here." Since he was in the great Tholing Monastery, Atisha made a pilgrimage to the many temples there, such as the temples of Chakrasamvara, Guhyusamaja, and so on. There were separate temples for sutra traditions and tantra traditions. Atisha was amazed to see the temples, and he observed that people were doing practice in each one, each according to the tradition of the temple. He noticed that they did not seem to know about practicing sutra and tantra together, so he questioned Rinchen Sangpo about his understanding of the sutras and tantras and how they are to be practiced. Rinchen Sangpo said he thought they each had to be practiced separately, according to their own tradition, without being mixed.

Atisha said, "I have found the reason for my having come on this long journey. In Tibet people don't know how to practice sutra and tantra traditions together, but I know how to do that and I can teach you how to practice them together. It is very important, because if one practices them separately, accomplishment is more difficult."

He explained that sutra and tantra conflict if they are not understood properly. The sutra methods deal with developing positivity, such as compassion; and abandoning negativity, such as anger. The tantric methods transform negative states into positive ones, and positive states into ultimate liberation, which is the essence of both positive and negative. From the tantric view, the presence or absence of positivity or negativity is not so significant, because negative and positive are seen as two sides of the same thing. Practicing the sutra method with tantric understanding or practicing the tantric method with sutra understanding is an excellent combination which will result in a beneficial fruition many times greater than may be achieved by practicing one tradition alone.

A story of a different kind of encounter is told about the great yogi Milarepa. Milarepa had an eventful life. He first studied to become a sorcerer, was successful at it, and used his powers to take revenge on some people. He then had remorse and eventually came to study and do meditation practice under Marpa Lotsawa in order to purify his negative actions. After many years of solitary meditation people began to come to him to learn, and he taught them with songs that he improvised according to the occasion. He was not famous for his mastery of ordinary logic but for his skill in utilizing those same principles in a spontaneous and unorthodox manner. His ability came not from defeating others in debate but from the realization he attained after many years of dedicated study and practice of vajrayana teachings. There are many stories about people who challenged Milarepa, from sorcerers to demonesses. In the story of Lotön and Tarlo, two scholars who came to dispute with Milarepa on the grounds of logic, Milarepa demonstrated that he was highly accomplished in the vajrayana method of transcending the rigidity produced by ego-based learning. Lotön and Tarlo were learned scholars who, jealous of Milarepa's fame and many followers, began talking against him. They called him a heretic and maintained that he had no learning; they criticized him for teaching other people while having no knowledge of the fine points of logic and dharma that they themselves had. One day they decided to go and dispute with him face to face. When they met Milarepa, they asked him what teachings he knew. Milarepa replied that he knew the teachings he had been given by his guru, Marpa Lotsawa. They asked what kind of proof he had, in logical terms, to substantiate the teachings that he practiced and taught. The kinds of proof they asked for are traditionally called "signs of contradiction" and "signs of establishment." Milarepa replied, "The proof I have for the sign of contradiction is that your minds are in contradiction with the dharma because you don't practice the dharma, therefore you are in contradiction with it. The same word that means establishment can also mean practice, so my sign of practice is that I am able to practice the dharma."

When he said that, Lotön and Tarlo both laughed, saying, "That is a sign that you don't understand the dharma. That is not what is meant by the terms proof and refutation. Also, you say that people like us who do know the dharma are at fault. What you are doing is in contradiction to the dharma."

So Milarepa said, "I'll ask you some questions. Is space obstructive or unobstructive?"

"Everyone knows that space is not obstructive. There isn't even any need to ask such a question. It is obvious that space is not obstructive."

"Are you sure?"

"Yes, of course."

"Well, if it is not obstructive, then move about in space right now." When they tried to move they couldn't move, all they could do was sit there and look.

Milarepa said, "So you see, space is obstructive."

When they recovered from their shock they accused Milarepa of creating an illusion, saying, "Everyone knows that space is unobstructive and it says so in all the Buddha's teachings and all the commentaries. You are using magic."

Milarepa again asked, "How about a wall? Is that materially obstructive or not?" They answered that a wall is obstructive. Then Milarepa passed through the wall.

By conducting a dispute in this way, Milarepa made the

point to the two scholars that whether a thing is solid or not solid is not the important thing. The point is that everything is empty. He also demonstrated the limitations of knowledge that is not accompanied by the understanding and realization that comes with training the mind through contemplation. In such a debate no conclusions may be drawn because relatively things are always changing. One who, like Milarepa, has clarified the mind to such an extent that the essential nature of the elements and the universal laws are fully known can play with the elements as Milarepa did and demonstrate the illusory nature of reality and, through that, its essential emptiness.

The Buddha himself encouraged using every means to discover and understand truth. At one point he told a group of his disciples, "You must examine my words to their very depths, then test what I say as you would test gold, and having so tested and proven the validity and truth of what I say for yourselves, only then should you accept it." That is the spirit of logic, and that is how it is applicable in practical life. Most people, unless they are philosophy professors, do not have the time to develop esoteric arguments. What we are all concerned with every day, however, is living life effectively, according to reliable methods that take into account the well-being of others as well as ourselves. To do this we must be awake and alert, not accepting something we hear just because we heard it or because it flatters us somehow, but using our faculties of discrimination to find out for ourselves if it is acceptable or not. The science of truth assists us in this process of weighing things impartially, with a scale of accuracy that is unhindered by our own subjective desire, aversion, pride, jealousy, or anger.

Though a complicated subject like Buddhist logic may at first glance seem irrelevant to anything we have to do in an average day, in actuality it is another, finer link between the relative world and ultimate mind. It is a refinement of wisdom that progressively simplifies things until the point where the individual can take the leap from refined relative action and understanding into the ultimate beyond, which is complete enlightenment.

9
INNER TRUTH

*Profound wisdom arises
from insight.*

INNER TRUTH IS THE HEART OF ALL knowledge, and it is the most significant result that can come from diligent study of the branches of ordinary and extraordinary knowledge. All these disciplines are avenues that lead in their various ways to inner truth, the highest level of knowledge, a level of realized wisdom that is beyond intellectual concepts. Knowing inner meaning is the key to everything, and mastering any of the branches of knowledge can lead to this kind of wisdom. When any path of knowledge is developed in the right way and developed completely, that refined knowledge becomes wisdom, insight, and inner truth.

There is one branch of knowledge, however, that explores and develops inner truth with the specific aim of achieving its fullest, most complete realization. This is the profound and most extraordinary discipline of inner knowledge. There are important reasons why inner knowledge should require a special study all to itself. Inner truth is not the same as relative truth. It incorporates the understanding of ultimate truth, in which all individuals and circumstances, despite their relative appearances, are known to be perfect. From the standpoint of inner knowledge there are no individuals who are not perfect ultimately; imperfection is but a relative manifestation. Gaining this depth of comprehension of the universe and actually making it a part of oneself takes a different kind of effort than that demanded by other branches of knowledge. In developing inner knowledge, the focus is on various forms of mind training, meditation, and other practices that stimulate deeper levels of awakening to truth.

All aspects of knowledge are aimed at correcting imperfections of the relative state and finally unveiling the perfection of the ultimate nature of every individual. These disciplines not only reveal but generate recognition and realization of this profound truth. At this point of realization the relative world is fully known to coexist with ultimate mind. This is the departure point for the path of inner knowledge.

Maintaining the correct view allows you to operate in the right way in your life. A correct relationship with all the things you encounter day to day is the purpose of practices like meditation. These, when done properly, will maintain the correct view. This foundation will beneficially influence every aspect of life activity. The two principles of view and practice function not only in the sphere of mantras and meditation but also in the sphere of filing a report or preparing a meal. Correct view and practice together will bear the fruit that is liberation, realization, or, to put it another way, ultimate perfection. Ultimately there is no imperfection and relatively there is no perfection, so through relative imperfection one can journey toward ultimate perfection. This perfection is not something you create but something that is to be liberated from the relative world, where it is inherent. It is liberated by the play of universal principles in the impermanent, relative world. When you gain consciousness and later mastery of these principles, when you have the correct view, everything else will follow.

Development of inner knowledge is done most effectively through the means of meditation. Even though the inner essence of everyone is perfect, external conditions and manifestations of perfection are often lacking. Some perfect qualities may manifest, but the manifestation of totally realized inner knowledge is a rare event. Meditation practice makes it possible to gradually overcome imperfect conditions and liberate the inner quality of perfection. Meditation is the most powerful way to do this. Many methods of meditation are taught and practiced—methods that are suitable for different individuals at different stages of development and for specific purposes. Not everything can be done at once. Complete realization must be built up slowly, by clarifying the body, speech, and mind in various ways and then by stabilizing this clarity. That is why such a tremendous number of methods are given.

All meditation methods bring results if you have a firm foundation. The development of this foundation involves two basic practices: *shinay* or "tranquillity meditation," and *lhathong*, or "insight meditation." The term shinay means reaching the state of mind that is calm, harmonious, and free from disturbing thoughts and defilements. On that basic condition, the condition of a calm mind, one then develops lhathong, which adds clarity, sharpness, and ability for profound observation. After considerable development of shinay and lhathong, the meditation practitioner reaches the perfect state of harmony. When this state of harmony is reached, defilements and confusions naturally dissolve. A person who practices this method will, at the beginning, experience a temporary result: a state of perfect harmony, in which things can be seen clearly and defilements can be purified. But this result will not be stable at first. A person who continues this practice will reach a stage of accomplishment in which the perfect harmonious state will last longer. With further effort, it is possible to retain this state at all times and remain in the experience of perfect harmony in every moment of life. If you are at that stage of accomplishment and come across a negative situation that is confusing, depressing, or damaging, instead of the situation affecting you, you will be able to affect it, for the better. When clarity is stabilized and habitual, the clear-minded person has the ability to overcome negative influences and conditions. It is possible to change a negative condition, and even to influence another person to become more positive and harmonious. This is the result of diligent shinay and lhathong meditation.

The shinay and lhathong state of mind can lead to a high state of realization, which is one of the highest states, called *du sem tse chikpa*, which might be translated as "perfectly realized human being." It is a condition of being natural, in which the individual cannot do anything wrong but naturally does the appropriate thing. It is the most profound state of mind achievable by a human being in the human physical, environmental, and psychological condition that we know. It is an extremely high level of intelligence, wisdom, and clarity, and it is the ultimate state of advancement that an ordinary human being can reach. Further developments can take place, but these are not considered to be within the sphere of ordinary human conditions. Within the human realm, *du sem tse chikpa* is the highest level of consciousness that can be achieved, and it can be achieved through shinay and lhathong meditation.

To go further than that is to have the realization of the ultimate essence of mind itself, which is actually the goal of the pursuit of inner knowledge. Again, there are many methods to achieve this, but one of the most profound methods is recognition of the mind (*sem ngo tokpa*). If a person can recognize the nature of mind, in the particular state of the perfected, advanced human being, then the person's innermost essence, the limitless potential, will be liberated. That is the achievement of what is termed the first level of the bodhisattva. In that state a person can have tremendously powerful and positive immediate manifestations as well as guaranteed further realizations. These realizations are described as the ten successive levels of bodhisattva realization, ending with the final liberation of the buddha, the ultimate state of realization which has no limitation whatsoever. Although the realization of a first-level bodhisattva has limitations compared to the levels of realization yet to be achieved, it is limitless when compared to the state of ordinary beings. It is a tremendous advance in realization that is not easy to describe. The texts define a first-level bodhisattva as someone who can manifest one hundred perfect manifestations at once. Ordinary, undeveloped human beings have a hard time manifesting one profoundly, even for five minutes, because of the defilements, confusion, delusion, and misunderstanding that make up their limited world. The first-level bodhisattva is perfect, free from the limitations of ordinary human beings. *Du sem tse chikpa,* the perfected human being, is considered to be a perfect manifestation, also free from limitations and from which there is no falling back. The study of inner truth is the profoundest study of all, because it is the way of inner development and includes every form of mind-training method and meditation. Inner knowledge involves the search for, and the development of, the many facets of inner truth through specialized methods of meditation. Inner knowledge is necessary, essential, and relevant to every single living being, because each sentient being's ultimate potential is unlimited. Due to this limitless potential, no sentient being will rest in contentment until liberation of this potential is reached. Sentient beings will go on making mistakes, making progress, and having problems, no matter what, until they reach the unlimited freedom that enlightenment brings. Liberation starts when a being achieves *du sem tse chikpa.* Final liberation is buddahood. The essential, unlimited buddha-nature drives everyone, all sentient beings, to find the way out of their limited condition. Even the most ignorant will not be satisfied by anything, though they may not know why. Everybody runs around like ants, not knowing why. If asked what they want, nobody knows. That question will not be answered, the search will not end, nor will beings be fulfilled, until they reach ultimate liberation. Sentient beings will stop suffering only when they reach unlimited, enlightened freedom that is gained through inner development.

This search and struggle leads to the core of inner truth, and Buddhist teachings offer methods that greatly assist and simplify the search. Shinay meditation consist of such methods as awareness of breathing or constant observation of particular images or sounds. These help the individual to stabilize the mind. They replace crowded thoughts that hinder the person's ability to see things clearly with tranquility, and with that the ability to relate to life's circumstances with more clarity of mind. The person begins to have less distracting thoughts and more continuous awareness. Building on that initial achievement, the meditator can maintain longer periods of calmness with both physical and mental activities. When this is mastered, lhathong may be practiced: one observes this calmness and quietness with clarity. Tranquillity, clarity, and sharp observation result from the combination of shinay and lhathong. With these tools an individual can progress further. The clarity will continue to clarify, and greater depth of understanding will be possible. One will have an increasing ability to maintain harmonious physical and mental conditions, as well as harmony in relation to both internal and external circumstances.

Advanced techniques in the study of inner knowledge may utilize vizualization and symbolism, which are sometimes very complex. Seeing the universe in different arrangements is another way to deepen understanding. The transformation of relative states of consciousness into an understanding of ultimate mind is described in the esoteric vajrayana teachings related to the five buddha families. These teachings are an example of the meaning that can lie within the ordinary. They describe the five directions, elements, and other phenomena of the relative world as expressions of the path to enlightenment as followed in Tibetan Buddhism. Following is one well-known interpretation of these teachings; the association of elements, colors, and directions sometimes varies if a particular emphasis is required for a teaching or practice.

East, the direction of sunrise, is associated with the element water and the color white. Its season is winter. The defilement associated with this direction is aggression, and its ultimate potential, when the aggression is transformed, is mirrorlike wisdom. What this means is that emptiness is like a mirror of all phenomena; everything is reflected in it. When defilements are overcome, all can be clearly seen and known. East is associated with the vajra, or adamant, family of Buddha Akshobhya. Its mantra is HUM.

South is associated with the element earth and the color yellow. Its season is autumn. Its defilement is ego, or pride, which is transformed into the wisdom of equanimity—the realization of freedom from duality. South is associated with the ratna, or jewel, family of Buddha Ratnasambhava. Its mantra is TRAM.

West is associated with the element fire and the color red. Its season is spring. Its defilement is attachment and desire, which is transformed into discriminating wisdom. Discriminating wisdom is experienced as the realization that all phenomena, with form and without form, have unconfused qualities. West is associated with the padma, or lotus, family of Buddha Amitabha. Its mantra is HRI.

North is associated with the element air and the color green. Its defilement is jealousy, which, when transmuted, becomes all-accomplishing wisdom. The ultimate essence of samsara and nirvana are understood as one, not two different things. North is associated with the karma family of Buddha Amoghasiddhi. Its mantra is TA.

The center is also considered a direction, associated with the element space and the color blue. Its defilement is ignorance which is transmuted into limitless, or all-encompassing, wisdom. It is dharma space, within which everything manifests beyond time and limitation. It is associated with the buddha family of Buddha Vairochana, and its mantra is OM.

The buddha families are one example of how ordinary reality is linked to a truth that transcends all ordinary knowledge and activity. An individual's actual development is an awakening to inner truth. This awakening is brought about through mental discipline interrelated with physical discipline. The mental principle is that everyone's mind is ultimately perfect, everyone's mind has the complete ability to understand itself and everything else, everyone's mind has absolute power over phenomena. But temporary defilements—ignorance, pride, anger, desire, and jealousy—handicap the ability to understand. These mental states maintain each other and obscure recognition of the inner truth that lies within them. They manufacture as their by-products endless distracting thoughts and emotions, such as attachment, aversion, and aggression.

The more deeply the practitioner becomes involved in the pursuit of inner knowledge, the less comprehensible the teachings become to ordinary mind. This can be demonstrated by stories from the texts about vajrayana masters, which often include inspirational songs, called dohas. These songs do not always make much sense to the ordinary mind.

The yogi Tilopa received one such song from a dakini, a female celestial being, in a vision. The dakini told him:

> The meaning of meaning will not be understood through the
> meaning of word.
> Water washes the stain but water does not wash water itself.
> A committed person with exceptional intelligence
> Can overcome the bondage of external liberation
> And can hold the ultimate inner liberation.
> One must apply the great ever-present method free of all
> limitation.

In another story, even harder for ordinary mind to understand, Tilopa shows his extraordinary powers. One day at a gathering with a number of pandits and yogins, Tilopa performed a miracle: in each hair follicle of his body he manifested a mandala, which is the representation of the environment of a meditational deity. The mandala did not appear small, and the body did not appear large. He sang a song about this "unthinkable miracle" beyond ordinary comprehension:

> If you sit, sit in the middle of the sky.
> If you sleep, sleep on the point of a spear.

If you look, look upon the center of the sun.
I, Tilopa, who realized the ultimate, am the one who is free
   of all effort.

Vajrayana teachings and practices confront our fixed limitations from every angle. It is not easy in the relative world
to get rid of negativity and extract what is positive because
of the paradoxical nature of the universe. Ultimately there is
nothing to obscure; ultimately there is nothing that can
obscure. But relatively there is everything to be obscured and
everything can become an obstacle. So at the same time that
there is no such thing as ultimate defilement, a defilement is
there, indeed, and it is there in a most peculiar way, because
you can't put your finger on it. You can't say it is there. You
can't say it is not there. Ultimately it has never been there.
Relatively it has always been there. Ultimately there is nothing
to purify and there is nothing to clarify. Relatively there is
everything to be purified. Even the method of purification
itself is an obscuration that has to be shed later on.

It is like the soap and water you use to wash your dirty
clothes. Soap and water are necessary while you are washing
the clothes, but once the clothes are clean the soap and water
become as undesirable as the dirt, so the garment must be
rinsed and dried before it is ready. Though inner awakening
is not exactly the same as laundering clothes, the analogy
might give an approximate idea. Thoughts that are used for
development on the path to inner awakening—thoughts like
compassion, devotion, and dedication—become spontaneously manifest beyond concept once the awakening actually
takes place.

Events are governed by similar principles. Ultimately no
events are imperfect, and relatively no events are perfect.
Therefore, until liberation it is vital that constant mindfulness
and awareness be maintained in relation to any event. This is
the way one's view becomes realistic, useful, and practical

rather than remaining as no more than an idealistic, grandiose concept disconnected from life.

Once you understand the principles, you must apply them to reality—the relative world. That is the practice. You deal with yourself, with others, and with situations using these principles. Through various methods that resemble the basic common sense of human beings, you strive to be a truthful, helpful, kind, and genuine human being. You practice by being kind, both to yourself and others; by being helpful, both to yourself and to others; and by not abusing yourself or others. It is from the level of day-to-day reality that one deals with all levels of development, physical and mental. All activity is practice, even if it merely involves getting up in the morning, eating, and sleeping. If all you do is that, it is still practice. Even doing nothing is practice, and according to your skill in applying the principles, according to your attitude and motivation, your practice becomes either beneficial or harmful. Appropriate mind training and meditation practice are essential on the path of inner knowledge. All of these things together—right view and the application of it in life situations, united with the effort to gain inner knowledge through contemplation and discipline of mind—will develop true inner wisdom. Once you develop and establish inner wisdom it will gradually take you to the final stage of enlightenment, which is a final realization—not just a temporary flash of realization about a relative thing, but the ultimate liberation. Enlightenment, after all, is not a one-sided accomplishment; enlightenment is a central accomplishment.

How to establish inner truth is, in itself, an enormous subject of study, but it is through disciplines of knowledge in practical life that one liberates this most profound essence which is inherent in everything. When Buddha Shakyamuni taught twenty-five hundred years ago, he did not call his ideas Buddhism, but he used a word of which the Tibetan equivalent is *nang*, "the interior" or "inner." Why did he use such a term? There is an ultimate essence, which is always perfect and limitless, within everything and everyone, and his teaching is about that essence. Presenting the means to discover it in everything, to use it, and to liberate it was the purpose of all the Buddha's teaching. That is why he referred to the inner meaning. All aspects of ordinary and extraordinary knowledge are connected to this crown of all knowing, inner truth.

When Tilopa gave Naropa his final teaching, he asked him to perform a difficult and elaborate offering ceremony. After it was concluded Naropa, not satisfied with the profoundest of teachings his guru had bestowed upon him, showed his lack of full realization by asking for deeper teachings.

On hearing this, Tilopa looked around in fury for something to beat him with and found his sandal. He picked up the sandal and struck Naropa hard on the face. Naropa lost consciousness, but when he awoke, he awoke enlightened. Tilopa sang this song:

This is the self-recognition of wisdom.
It is not subject to the activities of speech and mind.
I have nothing to show.
One's own ultimate essence is recognized by one's own self.

NOTES

EDITOR'S FOREWORD

1. This is a simplified listing. The traditional list as given by Jamgön Kongtrül Lodrö Thaye comprises what are known as "the eight great wooden chariots of the practice lineage" and includes Nyingmapa, Kadampa, Lamdre, Marpa Kagyü, Shangpa Kagyü, Shije, Bujo, and Dorje Nyendrup.
2. "The Song of Chokyi Jungne," *Rain of Wisdom* (Boulder and London: Shambhala Publications, 1980).

CHAPTER 2. HEALING THE BODY

1. The six realms of the cycle of existence are the higher realms of the gods, jealous gods, and humans; and the lower realms of the animals, hungry ghosts, and hell beings. In the Buddhist view, the most fortunate birth is in the human realm, because the versatility of human consciousness gives more opportunity for liberation from the suffering and bondage of this cycle.

CHAPTER 3. HEALING THE MIND

1. *Samsara* is a Sanskrit word for the cycle of existence, which is characterized by successive rebirth, caused by ignorance, in realms of inevitable suffering.

CHAPTER 4. LANGUAGE

1. *Punyabala-avadaana-sutra,* Rumtek Kangyur, vol. 76, p. 3.

2. *Arya-brahma-paripriccha-nama-mahayana-sutra,* Rumtek Kangyur, vol. 59, p. 5.

3. *Skandha* is a Sanskrit term for what are known as the five aggregates of experience: form, feeling, perception, formation, and consciousness.

4. *Arya-mahalalika-paripriccha-nama-mahayana-sutra,* Rumtek Kangyur, vol. 59, p. 621.

5. *Vajra-daka-nama-uttara-tantra,* Rumtek Kangyur, vol. 78, p. 251.

6. *Shri-maha-samvarodaya-tantra-raja,* Rumtek Kangyur, vol. 78, p. 53.

7. *Vinaya-karika,* Rumtek Tengyur, vol. 166, p. 192.

8. *Arya-mula-sarvastivadi-shramanera-karika,* Rumtek Tengyur, vol. 59, p. 125.

9. Ibid., p. 138.

10. *Udanvarga,* Rumtek Tengyur, vol. 148, p. 30.

11. Ibid., p. 230.

12. Ibid., p. 401.

13. *Samantamukha-pravesha-rashmi-vimaloshnisha-prabhasa-sarvatathagata-hridaya-samayavilokita-nama-dharani,* Rumtek Tengyur, vol. 90.

CHAPTER 5. POETRY

1. The blue utpala flower is common in poetic descriptions.

2. The phurba is a ceremonial dagger.

3. The tamboura is a stringed Indian musical instrument that is strummed to provide background for voice or other instruments.

4. The four maras are four difficulties encountered on the path: defilements, impermanence, death, and attachment.

CHAPTER 7. ASTROLOGY AND GEOMANCY

1. In the Buddhist conception of the ideal universe, Mount Meru, which occupies the central point, is surrounded by the ocean, seven rings of mountains, seven lakes, the sun and moon, various levels, palaces, and other features representing the whole of phenomenal existence. Ancient Buddhist temples were sometimes built according to this mandala of the universe: e.g., Borobudur in Java, Ankor Wat in Cambodia, Shwe Dagon in Rangoon, and Samye Monastery in Tibet.

CHAPTER 8. SCIENCE OF TRUTH

1. *Parinirvana* is a Sanskrit term describing the complete cessation of the cycle of rebirth for an enlightened being.

INDEX

Abhidharma, 74
Aesthetic mood, 81, 93
    in music, 93
    in poetry, 81
Aggression, 138
    mirrorlike wisdom and, 138
Air influence, 24–26
    symptoms of imbalance, 25–26
Akbar (Mughal emperor), 92
Anger, 50–53, 56
    mental illness and, 29–30
Astrology, 5, 97–108, 112
    geomancy and, 108–112
    mathematics and, 97–98, 112
    Tibetan, 99–108
Atisha Dipankara, *xii*, 124–125
Attachment, 50–52, 74, 139
    to body, 57
    discriminating wisdom and, 139
    mental illness and, 29–30
Awareness, 74

Bile influence, 24–26
    symptoms of imbalance, 25, 26
Bodhisattva(s), *xv*, 136
    first level, 136–137
    ten levels of, 136

Body-speech-mind, 6–7
    language and, 75–76
    sacred dance and, 91
    sound and, 6
Bön religion, *viii, xi, xiv*
Book of Changes, 105–108
Brahma, 71
Breathing, 55
    balancing, 55, 57
    cleansing, 58
Buddha-nature, 137
Buddha Shakyamuni, *ix*, 1, 128, 142
    enlightenment of, 3, 5
    parinirvana of, 120, 147n.8.1
    teachings of, 1–3, 48, 70–76, 128, 142–143
Buddhism, 142
    Chittamatrin school, 120–121
    hinayana, *ix, x–xi*
    mahayana, *ix, xv*
    persecution of, *xi–xii*, 124
    Sautrantika school, 120–121
    Vaibashika school, 120–121
    vajrayana (tantric), *x*, 53–60, 69, 141
    See also Sutra and tantra traditions; Tibetan Buddhism

Index

Index

Index

Negativity, 42, 43, 46, 141
Ngönjö (study of names), 69
Nyingmapa lineage, xi

Oral transmission, xii
Ordinary aspects of knowledge
  astrology, 97–112
  grammar, 5, 67–69
  names, 5, 69, 79
  performance, 5, 89–94
  poetry, 5, 79–86

Padmasambhava, viii, ix, xi
Painting, 14–15
Parinirvana, 120, 147n.8.1
Parkha (Tibetan Book of
  Changes), 105–108
  trigrams in, 106–107
Path, 74–75
Perfect form, 13–14, 21
Perfection, 13, 21, 134
  relative world and, 134
Performance, 5, 89–94
  daily life as, 94
  music as, 92–93
  sacred, 89–92
  secular, 91
Phlegm influence, 24–27
  symptoms of imbalance, 25,
  26–27
Phurba, 83, 146n.5.2
Poetry, 5, 79–86
  aesthetic moods of, 81
  kinds of, 80–86
  meaning and sound in, 79
  rules of, 80–86
  subject of, 79–86

Potala Palace (Lhasa), 111
Pottery, 14
Prayer. See Mantra
Pregnancy, 38
Pride, 53–54
  wisdom of equanimity and, 139
Psychotherapy, 38
  See also Therapy
Pulse diagnosis, 28–29

Rama, 84
Relative truth, 3, 117–119
  inner truth vs., 133
  language as, 75
Relative world, 42
  perfection and, 134
  ultimate mind and, 3–5, 7, 18,
  128–129, 134
Rinchen Sangpo, Lotsawa, xii,
  124–125

Sacred dance, 89–92
Sacred words, 69
  See also Mantra
Sakyapa lineage, xiii, xvi
Samsara, 42, 74–75, 84–85,
  145n.3.1
Sautrantika school, 120–121
Science of truth, 5, 117–129
Self-hatred, 42–43
Shantarakshita (Khenpo Bodhis-
  ato), viii, 122–123
Shinay (tranquility) meditation,
  49, 135–136, 137–138
Shunyata, ix–x
  See also Emptiness

Index

Index